a gift

EOIH'S VOICE IN THE WIND

*A Guide to Higher Consciousness
and Life After Death*

Anne apRoberts

BALBOA.
PRESS

A DIVISION OF HAY HOUSE

Balboa Press books may be ordered through booksellers or by contacting:

Balboa Press
A Division of Hay House
1663 Liberty Drive
Bloomington, IN 47403
www.balboapress.com
1 (877) 407-4847

Print information available on the last page.

ISBN: 978-1-5043-4086-1 (sc)
ISBN: 978-1-5043-4088-5 (hc)
ISBN: 978-1-5043-4087-8 (e)

Library of Congress Control Number: 2015915510

Balboa Press rev. date: 11/30/2015

For Elizabeth Shuey
Who had the courage and the vision to follow spirit.
And Dr. John Newbrough
Who asked the deeper questions.

Acknowledgements

My deep appreciation to Mr. Phoenix Luck Steen for all his support and encouragement and long hours of proofreading this book.

Thank you J.B. for your priceless help with editing.

My gratitude to Elizabeth Shuey for pointing me toward the wisdom of the Oahpse.

Around and through it all, my humble gratitude to the unseen ones who have given me the courage and tenacity to create this book.

EOIH: The Creator
Pronounced: E...O...E

Chief over all that live on the earth I made Man; male and female I made them. And that Man might distinguish Me, I commanded them to give Me a name; by virtue of My presence I commanded them. And Man named Me not after anything in heaven or on the earth. In obedience to My will they named Me after the sounds the wind uttered, and they said, E-O-IH!

As the wind whispers E in the leaves, and utters O in the ocean's surge and in the thunder above, and Ih in the winter's shrill whistle, so came the name E-O-Ih, which has become Jehovih, and Eloih, and Elohim and Wenohim.

— Both Quotes from the Oahspe 1925

OAHSPE: Earth, Sky, and Spirit
Pronounced: O...Aa...Spe

Contents

I. Oahspe 1

Describing the seven eras of mankind's development from the creation of Man to the present time.

> *Not infallible is this book, the Oahspe, but to teach mortals how to attain to hear the Creator's voice and to see His heavens in full consciousness, while still living on the earth; and to know of a truth the place and condition awaiting them after death.*

– All Quotes from the 1925 Published Edition of The Oahspe

II. The Voice of Man 11

An apology and a plea for the Creator to help and speak to humanity.

> *Where have I invented one thought but by looking upon Your works? How can I otherwise than remember my Creator, and out of Your creations, O Creator, find rich food for meditation all the days of my life? And yet, though I have appropriated the earth to myself, I am neither happy nor perfect overall. Misery and crime and selfishness are upon my people.*

III. *The Book of Jehovih*............17

Here is revealed how this world was created, where the heavens are and the life and work of the spirits of the dead.

He said, I am the soul of all, and the all that is seen is of My person and is My body.

IV. The Book of Ben

This section is sometimes called the "Book of the Nine Entities, Who Are the Tree of All Light."

> *Jehovih said: All power I gave to the unseen to rule over the seen. Kosmon said: Why wilt you, O Man, search forever in corpor for the cause of things? Behold, the unseen part of yourself rules over the seen.*

V. The Book of Judgment..93

Being the grades and rates of mortals and angels in the light of God, as the Word came to Es, Daughter of the Creator.

Nor have I come to say: Behold, this is my book! And there will be none other! But, behold, I come to found Creator's kingdom on earth. I come to the wise and learned, and not to one person only; but to thousands. That which I am uttering in these words, in this place, I am also uttering in the souls of thousands, and I will bring them together.

VI. The Book of Inspiration.................................193

The Creator describes Himself.

I am to your spirit, as is the sun to a ray of light. I am the Light that illuminates your soul. The ray of light that goes out of Me takes root in mortality, and you are the product, the tree.

VII. The Book of Discipline...................223

God reveals who he is.

> *Hear the words of your God, O Man—I am your brother, risen from mortality to a holy place in heaven: Profit in my wisdom and be admonished by my love. For as I am your elder brother, so will it be with you, to raise also in time to come, and look back to mortals and call them to the exalted heavens of the Creator.*

Illustrations

About the Order of the Trees

The Order of the Trees was formed in 1975 under the auspices of the Oahspe Foundation, a non-profit 501(c) 3 religious corporation located in Oregon. The Order of the Trees is a spiritual community that seeks to live the tenants of the Oahspe. The Order of the Trees lives in southern Oregon at the Eloin Wilderness Preserve, which is owned and operated by the Oahspe Foundation.

Our day-to-day practices consist of living self-sufficiently and ecologically in the wilderness, with a focus on healthy living and spiritual development. We consider ourselves a model of possibility. Our community is composed of men, women and children of all ages, who contribute their time and energy to manifest the seeds of possibility that create harmony and understanding and a reverence for all Life.

For further information please visit our website at: www.eloinforest.org

The Main Speakers in Eoih's Voice in the Wind

The Creator is referred to as: *Jehovih, The Creator, the I AM, Eoih, Divine Presence, Great Spirit, the Ever Present,* and *All Light,* to name the most often used in this text.

The angelic being who rules our world is called *God* or *Goddess,* not to be confused with the Creator. This being is a onetime mortal who evolved to a level of consciousness in which he (or she) is capable of managing the spiritual and corporeal realms of this world. The God/Goddess of this world works with a holy council and millions of other spirit beings.

All capitalized versions of He, His or Him, and My refer to the Creator.

All capitalized versions of Man refer to mankind or humanity.

Preface

The first time I was introduced to the Oahspe, I read the first few pages and handed it back to my friend and said, "I just left organized religion. No Thanks." He tried to tell me that it wasn't about organized religion, but I wasn't listening. I was preparing to leave the world I was born in and grew up in. I was trying to find my way out of a life that didn't make sense to me anymore. I was looking for the doorway into a life of purpose and deeper meaning, a life filled with possibilities of peace and justice for all people. It was 1975, and I knew in my heart that life was meant to be lived for the sake of goodness and the upliftment of all life on this extraordinary planet.

All my life I have had a deep connection to spirit. The voice has helped me many times, and in 1972 it was guiding me out of one world and into another. Diagnosed with a life-threatening disease at the age of 23, I was not willing to hand myself over to a surgery that would damage me for the rest my life. The voice guided me to health food stores and told me what books to read to learn about herbs and diet, and a whole new way of life that was strange to me, and yet it made sense.

Then the spirit voice told me the date I was to leave my old world behind: April 13, 1975. Spirit has an odd sense of humor and often leaves out essential details. *Where was I going?* I've learned that following spirit is a bit like an Easter egg hunt. One is led by clues and not usually by specific instructions. It's a clear case of, "Follow the yellow brick road."

I had the clues. My VW was packed and I had my sprout rake built into the back seat area. I left for San Diego, California with a brochure about a workshop by Professor Edmond B. Szekely, who wrote the *Essene Gospels of Peace*. I knew nothing about him except I liked his book. It was a life-changing event for me. I had felt alone on my quest because I hadn't really met too many people who thought like I did. But at the conference, I walked into a whole room full of people who did think like me, and I breathed a sigh of relief as I realized I wasn't crazy after all.

I left the conference two weeks later with a piece of paper someone had given me during our last session. It contained information about a woman who had purchased property in Oregon and was dedicating it to be an Essence community. I was on my way to find out what was next and whether this was where I was to give my life in service to the Divine. This was my quest: *Where can I best serve the Creator?*

A few days later, I was standing in front of the woman's door in Talent, Oregon, wondering what to say to her. The door opened and a vivacious lady stepped out and invited me in for dinner. She had beautiful, long, blond hair, and she was wearing high heels, a skirt, and lipstick. She looked rather like ZaZa Gabor! It was very confusing. I thought perhaps I had the wrong information, or had made a mistake about the cosmic clue I thought I'd received at the conference in San Diego. She didn't fit my picture of a spiritual person, but how appearances do deceive us!

The dinner conversation was way over my young head and I started to become afraid. Maybe this was a cult. I thanked everyone for dinner and let my hostess know I was leaving, but then she offered me a room for the night. *Let's see, my car or a soft bed?* The choice was easy. I overcame my fears and said, "Thank you for the room. I will be leaving in the morning."

The next day, as I was packing my backpack, the voice came again and said, "Stay." *Stay? I don't know these people. They could be crazy. I don't even know half of what they are talking about.* The message was repeated, "Stay." Then there was a knock on the door and my hostess popped her head in and said, "This room is available and you are welcome to stay. I think you'll like this area."

My hostess was Elizabeth Shuey, President of the Oahspe Foundation. On the third day of my stay, she handed me the Oahspe, and I was shocked to see that book again. I handed it back to her with a "No thanks. I'm not into organized religion anymore." She just laughed and took it back.

I stayed. I met wonderful people and loved the idea of an Essene community in the wilderness, where I could serve the earth and the people of the earth. Elizabeth turned out to be an extraordinary medium and a wonderful person whose life was completely dedicated to the Creator.

I worked my way into the Oahspe slowly. I could not deny the wisdom I found there. Years later, I found out that Elizabeth had been introduced to the Oahspe by Wing Andersen, who was the editor of the 1925 version of the Oahpse. Upon meeting Elizabeth, he gave the original plates for the book to her and asked her to carry on.

So here I am, forty years later, working in the gardens, helping with the meals, continuing the dream of living a life that is in harmony with the earth and with the people of the earth. Elizabeth has passed over and is free to continue her life beyond the burdens of this world. Now it is my turn to take the helm of this ship of dreams into the future.

I offer *Eoih's Voice in the Wind* as my gift to those who seek a higher life—a life of meaning and purpose beyond the mundane existence of this world—and for all who seek to awaken to the truth of who we are, individually and collectively.

May the wisdom in this book from the Creator inspire you to live the greatness of your soul and dance with the gods.

Anne apRoberts
Abbess of The Order of the Trees
Ashland, Oregon 2015

Introduction

Eoih's Voice in the Wind presents us with a perspective of life from the angelic point of view. It is a call from the Creator and our elder brothers and sisters in spirit to awaken and embrace our true destiny, which is the same as that of the gods. Our lives do indeed have a great purpose, no matter what our current occupation or situation on earth, because we are immortal *God Seeds* at the beginning of a remarkable and infinite journey into the Light.

The Creator calls us to move beyond the confines of the traditional religions without losing the wisdom contained within them, and to move past any teaching that encourages prejudice, separation, war, and domination. Humanity is moving into a new time and a new way of living and thinking. This is the time when we must live our good intentions, walk our talk, and be *willing* to move beyond self-centered existence.

Eoih's Voice in the Wind teaches us that the Creator is everything and everywhere in every moment. Creator is the quantum field. It is the Light within everything. It is within all time and space, and matter and non-matter and Creator has an intimate capacity to interact with every individual and all sentient life.

Eoih's Voice in the Wind teaches us how to hear the Creator's voice and distinguish the types of inspirations that come to us from the mortal world and from the spiritual realms.

The Oahpse Bible was written in 1882. It is approximately 900 pages. Of those 900 pages the majority is about the history of this world and mankind over the last 70,000 years. Within that history are many wonderful and wise stories of the unfoldment of Man. The information contained in Eoin's Voice in the Wind comes mostly from the last 200 pages of the Oahpse. These books are referred to as the essential or doctrinal books of the Oahpse.

Eoih's Voice in the Wind is an introduction to the wisdom of the Oahspe. It is a running commentary with quotes from the seven doctrinal books of the *Oahspe*. It is an easy read and will give you a taste of the message of the original writings.

The original *Oahspe* was "received" by Dr. John B. Newbrough from the Creator and God by means of automatic writing—actually you could say by automatic "typewriter." The interesting thing about Dr. Newbrough's experience is that he did not read the writings that came through him until the entire manuscript had been written. All he saw during this process were angelic hands over his on the typewriter. Dr. Newbrough was a *medium*, which means he was capable of receiving messages from the spiritual realms. You can read more about Dr. Newbrough's fascinating experiences in the back of the book.

We encourage you to read *Eoih's Voice in the Wind* in the order that it is presented, as each section contains information pertinent to the next section.

We have not altered the content of the 1925 version of *Oahspe*, except to modernize the language, and we have removed the numbered sentence sequence. If you find a word or concept you have difficulty with, please refer to the Glossary and the Index. There are blank pages at the end of each book for your convenience in making notes.

We have included drawings taken from *Oahspe*. These drawings were done by angelic beings while Dr. Newbrough was standing in front of the canvas. He did not hold the brush, but rather observed as an angelic hand held the brush and did the painting. We created the diagram explaining the levels of the heavens and their relationship to the earth in order to help explain the organization of the heavens according to Oahpse.

The text includes guidelines to show us how to live beyond war and suffering and greed. The Creator gives us a formula for overcoming our weaknesses and tells us that this world is destined to manifest humanities' highest potential—and that we are now at the beginning of the final unfolding of our highest destiny on earth. We are living in a time when all people will be faced with the truth of who they are and the extraordinary reality in which we live.

Eoih's Voice in the Wind explains the workings of the spiritual realms and how beings in spirit interact with mortals. Some angels live on the earth side-by-side with mortals, and some have evolved into realms of higher consciousness away from the earth. Life in spirit is the next step of our evolution into the infinite growth of our soul. Once we have evolved beyond our limited and selfish perspectives, and have dedicated ourselves to the service of all life, we will continue our journey away from the earth and into the universe in service to the Creator.

God describes himself as our elder brother, a onetime mortal, who is in service to the Creator. He talks about the lower spirits that live on the earth with mortals and interact with them. He explains about the higher spirits that uplift humanity and help to guide the evolution of mankind. God shows us how to live our lives so that we attract to ourselves highly evolved angels and learn to manifest peace, compassion, and wisdom. God explains what we must do to become aligned to the higher consciousness of the spiritual worlds around us. God says we have been praying: "Thy kingdom come...on earth as it is in heaven," and soon our prayers will be answered. Ready or not, here comes the Light.

DISCLAIMER: **This commentary on seven books from Oahspe does not necessarily reflect the perspectives of all the people who study Oahspe.**

Oahspe

Describing the Eras of Mankind's Evolution

Oahspe

The first section of the original Oahspe Bible is titled Oahspe. It is an overview of the eras of Man's evolution from the creation of Man to the present day. It begins with the creation of Man and continues through six eras to the seventh era of the present day, which is called the "Age of Kosmon." This history of Man is a rich and varied account of the evolution of consciousness through the cycles of light and dark that all planets such as our earth experience.

The appearance of Man on earth occurred approximately seventy-two thousand years ago. The sinking of the continent of Pan, which caused the great flood, occurred approximately twenty-four thousand years ago. Approximately nine thousand years ago, the first religion that anchored spiritual wisdom permanently on earth was given to Man.

Man: 72,000 years ago
The Great Flood: 24,000 years ago
The Great Prophets: Zarathustra of Persia about 9,000 years ago, Abraham, Brahma, Eawatah and Po about 6,000 years ago, Moses Capilya and Chine about 3,000 years ago. Ka-Yu (Confucius) and Sakaya (Buddha) about 2,500 years ago and Joshu about 2,000 years ago.

The First Era

In the First Era, Man was created and they were created differently from the animal kingdom:

> *That you will know you are the work of My hand, I have given you capacity for knowledge, power, and dominion.*

When the earth had reached a state of evolution in which all the elements were in place to create and sustain Man, the Creator "drove" the elements together in order to create Man. Throughout this book there are references to *vortexia*, they explain how the power of a vortex is used to drive elements together to create celestial bodies and different forms of matter. It was the power of vortexia that was used to drive the elements together to form the earth and all life, including Man. Esoteric physiology maintains the existence of a vortexian field around every person and all forms of matter.

The Second Era

In the Second Era, Man was lacking in intelligence. Man could not take care of themselves. The Creator called for volunteers from the angelic beings of other worlds to come and help uplift Man:

> *But Man was helpless; he understood not the voice of the Almighty; neither did he stand upright. And Creator called His angels, who were older than the earth, and He said to them: Go and raise Man upright and teach him to understand.*

Where did we come from? Science is still seeking the answer to explain how we evolved from the animal kingdom.

The Creator called out to a multitude of angels, who were once mortals on other worlds like the earth, and invited them to come and help with the beginnings of this world. The angels who came were those whose previous mortal lives had been cut short and lacked the wisdom of a mortal life. It was an opportunity for them to experience the feelings and challenges of being mortal. These angels cohabitated with Man and created a new race of immortal beings.

More of this event is explained in the Book of Jehovih, Chapter VI, and the Book of Inspiration, Chapter VI.

3

The Third Era

During the Third Era, Man was taught by the angels to live together in towns and cities:

> Creator said to the angels that were with Man: Behold, Man has multiplied on the earth. Bring them together and teach them to dwell in cities and nations.

As Man developed and organized, his sense of self increased. Man's consciousness had developed enough to become selfish. He began to separate himself and desire things for himself. This change brought on the fourth era.

The Fourth Era

During the Fourth Era, conditions changed, and mankind began to listen to the "beast," which refers to the small, self-centered, greedy part of Man. Mankind began to fear, hate, and destroy each other. Because of their lack of knowledge, the selfish part of Man rose up and took control:

> And in that same time the Beast rose up before Man, and spoke to him saying: Possess whatever you want, for all things are yours and are good for you. And Man obeyed the Beast, and war came into the world. This was the fourth era.

The Fifth Era

In the Fifth Era, mankind realized that the beast had tricked him and he began to reach out to find peace, but it was not to be found:

> *But the beast said: Think not I am come to send peace on the earth; I come not to send peace, but a sword. I come to set man at variance against his father, and a daughter against her mother. Whatever you find to eat, be it fish or flesh, eat it, taking no thought of tomorrow.*

> *Mankind became carnivorous and lost the ability to hear the Creator's voice, because his being had become dense and unreceptive like there was a stone lying upon his soul. Man could no longer hear the Creator nor believe in Him. And that was the fifth era.*

The following is not a statement against the wisdom held within religions.

It is an indictment against religious organizations for going against their original doctrines, which commanded them not to kill, to treat their neighbor as themselves, and to live lives of kindness and compassion.

And then mankind divided itself into four main divisions called the *heads of the Beast*. They were the major religions of that time:

> *And the names of the heads of the Beast were Brahmin, Buddhist, Christian, and Mohammedan.*

> *And they divided the earth, and apportioned it between themselves, choosing soldiers and standing armies for the maintenance of their earthly aggrandizement.*

The Sixth Era

In the Sixth Era, mankind descended into the darkness of war and selfishness and fear:

> *And Man, in service of the Beast, gave one-sixth of his life and his labor to war and standing armies; and one-third of his life he gave to dissipation and drunkenness. This was the sixth era.*

This was a big turning point for Man, and for the angels who were helping with Man's evolution. The four major religions that had been brought to the earth to uplift Man had turned their backs on the original teachings from the Creator. They chose power and destruction instead of peace and prosperity for everyone. These religions followed fear and selfishness in order to maintain dominion over the people. They set man against man and created armies to destroy their brothers and sisters.

The Seventh Era

In the Seventh Era, the call has gone forth from the Creator demanding that we cease fighting and stop destroying life:

> *Your Creator commands you to change from a carnivorous Man of contention to a herbivorous man of peace. The four heads of the Beast will be put away, and war will be no more on the earth.*

Changes reflecting the fulfillment of this demand from the Creator can be seen all around the earth. People are becoming more and more health conscious. People are standing up for the right to resist going to war:

> *The armies will be disbanded. And, from this time forward, whoever desires not to go to war, you will not force them, for it is the commandment of Your Creator.*

Demonstrations are happening around the world against war, unjust governments, greed, and the pollution of our environment. We are in a time of great change and upheaval. Yes, we still have war, but many people no longer march to the war cries of their governments.

The major religions of the world are changing. Some are losing power and members. New groups for worship and study outside of the traditional organizations are forming all over the world. The traditional religions are becoming more liberal and reaching out to relate to each other. The Creator asks us to stop living in separation and to embrace the oneness of divine presence within us all and around us all. The time of separate religions is over:

> *Neither will you have any God, or Lord, or Savior, but only the Creator! Him only will you worship henceforth forever. I Am sufficient to My own creations.*

In order for humanity to have the clarity and strength to rise above fear and selfishness we must be able to step away from selfishness and fear and decide that we will live in a new light of understanding. Throughout Eoih's Voice in the Wind we are shown how to step away and create a world of peace and prosperity for everyone. The people who choose this path are called Faithest because their faith is in the Creator:

> *And to as many as separated them from the dominion of the Beast, making these covenants to Me, have I given the foundation of My kingdom on earth.*

> *And all such people will be My chosen. By their covenants and by their works will they be known henceforth on the earth as Mine, and they will be called Faithists.*

> *But to as many as will not make these covenants, have I given the numbers of the Beast, and they will be called Uzians, signifying*

destroyers. And these will be henceforth the two kinds of people on earth, Faithists and Uzians.

An Uzian is someone who has faith in the Beast, which could also be defined as "materialist reality and a self-centered perspective." They might not believe in a spiritual existence, or they might believe in spirit, but their trust is in the war machine and their own desire and ability to succeed in the materialistic world:

But to as many as will not make these covenants, have I given the numbers of the Beast, and they will be called Uzians, signifying destroyers.

This division of humanity is not about religion, or any particular faith being better than another, or any race being superior to another. It's about the difference between builders and destroyers, and the growth and evolution of humanity away from fear, greed, and destruction. In the Seventh Era, we must learn to embrace and create a world of peace, happiness, and respect for the beauty and sacredness of all people and all life.

The seventh era began in the 1850s. It is called the Kosmon Era:

Because this light is comprehensive, embracing corporeal and spiritual things, it is called the beginning of the Kosmon Era. And because it relates to earth, sky and spirit, it is called Oahspe.

The beginning of this era is the beginning of a new time of light upon the earth and the angels come to earth to teach mankind a higher way of life:

And the angels of heaven descended to the earth to Man and appeared before him, face to face, hundreds of thousands of them, speaking as Man speaks, and writing as Man writes, teaching these things of Creator and His works.

The Creator tells us that books and philosophy and science are never the ultimate truth. These forms of learning are just that and they help us along the way, but only the presence of the divine in this moment holds truth:

Not infallible is this book, Oahspe,
but to teach mortals how to attain to hear the Creator's voice
and to see His heavens, in full consciousness,
while still living on the earth,
and to know of a truth the place and condition
awaiting them after death.

Neither are, nor were, the revelations within this Oahspe wholly new to mortals. The same things have been revealed at the same time to many, who live at remote distances from one another, but who were not in correspondence till afterward.

The Voice of Man

An Apology and a Plea for the
Creator to Help and to Speak

The Voice of Man

Man apologizes for humanities lack of ability to rise above the lower desires of the earth, and our inability to hold onto goodness and purity in the face of the lures of the world. The great lures of worldly experience often overwhelm our physical being so that we cannot hear our spirit. The simplicity of creation and the subtle presence of the divine can be missed in the presence of the things that offer us excitement, novelty, and instant gratification. We are born with the capacity to have all these experiences and sensations, but we often miss the deeper, more subtle and enriching experiences that await us when we look beyond the obvious things of the material world:

> *What is my weakness that I cannot overcome it? Or what is my strength that I succumb to the desires of the earth? I build up my belief and courage in You, but I do not know the way of my weakness; I stumble and fall. Am I made that I will be forever a reproof to myself and a censure to my own behavior?*

Man explains how war has turned people away from spirit. How war has accursed humanity by bringing hunger, suffering, and separation to the world and how selfishness has lured humanity away from spirit with glory, honor, riches, and power, which eventually leads to war. People have learned to be proud of fighting and killing. We have been taught to live from conflict. We fight in our families; we fight in business. We set schools against each other, races against each other, and countries against each other. We have learned to fear and distrust one another. Life on earth has become what we have made it:

> *Why have I vainly set up myself as the highest of Your works? My failures are worse than any other living creature under the sun. I cannot build my house in perfection like a bird's; my ingenuity cannot fashion a spider's net; I cannot sail up in the air like a bird, nor live in the water like the fish, nor dwell in harmony like the bee.*

Half of my offspring die in infancy; the multitudes of my household are quarrelers, fighters, drunkards, and beggars; the best of my sons and daughters are less faithful than a dog! I go forth to war, to slay my brother, even while Your wide earth has room for all. Yes, I accurse the earth with starvation and sin and untimely death.

Mankind progressed into believing that building kingdoms and taking over other countries to make bigger kingdoms was a good thing to do. Aggression and domination became more important than kindness and compassion and freedom:

I made great pretensions in a kingdom. I called out to my people, saying: We must have a kingdom. I showed them no reason for it, but I asked them take up arms and follow me for patriotism's sake. And yet what was patriotism? Behold, I made it as something greater than You and Your commandment: You shall not kill.

Now war is commonplace. It has become so normal that many people do not believe the earth will ever be without it as long as Man lives on earth:

They built me forts and castles and arsenals without number. I called to my people, saying: Come, behold the glory of my defenses which I built for you! And they gave me money and garrisons, and ships of war, and torpedoes, shouting: Hurrah for our country! We have faith in these things, but not in You our Creator.

Man was not designed to remain barbaric. We are divine beings in the process of awakening to our higher potential and this awakening of consciousness will require awareness and trust. We have to learn to trust each other again, and to trust the Creator. Awareness and trust are essential for humanity to evolve beyond war and suffering.

People do not want war, but how can we possibly live in peace? Thou shalt not kill is relegated to when it is convenient. Believing in the concept of "an eye for an eye" is used to justify aggression and destruction:

> *O that I had remained faithful with You, Creator! But I invented Gods for the glory of the evil one.*

> *In one place I called out to my sons and daughters, saying: "Be you Brahmins? Brahma saves whoever professes his name." In another place I said: Be you Buddhists? Buddha saves whoever calls on his name." In another place I said: "Be you Christians? Christ saves whoever calls on his name." In another place I said: "Be you Mohammedans? Whoever says: "There is but one God and Mohammed is his prophet," will have indulgence without sin.*

This last quote is about how Man has changed the religions to gain the support and control of the people and to set Man against Man. As a result, we have forgotten that war is not a necessity. Peace is a necessity and a requirement for the earth at this time in its evolution.

In order for us to live in peace, we need to know that our longing for peace and a life of higher purpose is not only possible, but it is our soul's destiny as divine beings. We must trust that we have the capacity to understand how to live in peace and harmony.

Toward the end of The Voice of Man is a summary of our world's great faults:

> *In vain I have searched for a plan of redemption, a plan that would make the earth a paradise, and the life of Man a glory to You, and a joy to him.*

> *But alas, the two extremes, riches and poverty, have made the prospect of a millennium a thing of mockery. For one person that is rich there are a thousand poor, and their interests are an interminable conflict with one another.*

Labor cries out in pain; but capital smites him with a heartless blow.

Nation is against nation; king against king; merchant against merchant; consumer against producer. Yea, Man against Man in all things upon the earth. Because the state is rotten, the politician feeds on that; because society is rotten, the lawyer and court have riches and sumptuous feasts, because the flesh of my people is rotten, the physician finds a harvest of comfort.

Man is asking for help, and each of us can do the same every day. Show us the way, Jehovih. Teach us the truth of who we are, and open our eyes to Divine Presence in everyone and everything. We all have the ability to relate to the divine around us in the beauty of a sunset; in the grandeur of the mountains; in the eyes of a child and in our own hearts. Every moment of every day offers us an opportunity to listen, to see, to feel the sacredness of life, and to live in ways that will create a better world for everyone:

Now, O Creator, I come to You! You hold the secret of peace and harmony and goodwill amongst mortals.

Give me of Your light, O Father! Show me the way of proceeding, and that war and crime and poverty may come to an end.

Open the way of peace and love and virtue and truth, that Your children may rejoice in their lives and glorify You and Your works forever.

The Book of Jehovih

Here is revealed the three great worlds, corpor, atmospherea, and Etherea. As in all other bibles, it is revealed that this world was created, and how the Creator created it. Behold, this bible reveals where these heavens are, and the manner and glory and work that the spirits of the dead enjoy, by which the wisdom, power, love, and glory of the almighty are magnified for the understanding of Man.

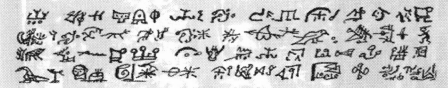

This is from the Panic language

'The universe is full; all things are members. Speech they have: Bid them speak. The recorder of their words be thou. Such is Panic (Earth) language, the first language. What says the bird? The beast? The stars? The sun? All? It is their souls speaking. Hear your soul, and repeat it. This light leads you to origin.'

The Creator Describes Himself - Chapter I

The Creator describes Himself as everything, not as a man or a woman, but as a force that is positive and therefore called *He*:

> *All was. All is. All ever will be. The All spoke and Motion was, and is, and ever will be; and, being positive, was called He and Him. The All Motion was His speech.*

The voice of the divine expresses itself within the motion of everything. That motion of all life is the music, the symphony of the Creator singing all life into being. The rush of the river, the wind underneath the wing, the dance of the trees and grass on a summer breeze, the roar of the ocean, and all the songs of life are the Creator's speech.

The Creator is the soul of everything, and the body of the Creator is in everything we see and experience. The earth, the trees, the stars, the oceans, the people, the creatures, and the galaxies are a part of the Great Spirit. We live within the Creator as a fish lives within the ocean, the Great Ocean of beingness in which we live and move:

> *He said, I am the soul of all and the all that is seen is of My person and is My body.*

The omnipresence of the Creator means we are never alone. There is nowhere to hide; there is no thought that is truly private; and there is no action that is unseen. We are not separate from the Creator. We are a part of the Creator, and as the famous quote from Desiderata says, "You are a child of the universe, no less than the trees and the stars."

The unseen rules the seen. The unseen is the potent or most powerful part of creation—the seen is the impotent part of creation. Scientists tell us that our five senses only perceive about five percent of reality.

If we only perceive five percent of reality, that pretty much leaves us in the dark about where we are and what is going on around us.

All matter is composed of particles that we cannot see with the naked eye. The motion of the atom is what holds life in form, determines the form, and is the energy of the form. Taking the unseen power a little further, most of us know that love, kindness, fear, and greed are powerful forces that literally rule the world. We also know that thoughts and feelings affect the world at the atomic level, as well. The subtle, or unseen, is the source of all we know:

> *Of two apparent entities am I, nevertheless I AM BUT ONE. These entities are the UNSEEN, which is POTENT, and the SEEN, which is of itself IMPOTENT and called CORPOR.*

> *With these two entities, in likeness thereby of Myself, I made all the living; for as the life is the potent part, so is the corporeal part the impotent part. Chief over all that live on the earth I made Man; male and female I made them.*

> *And that Man might distinguish Me, I commanded him to give Me a name; by virtue of My presence I commanded him. And Man named Me not after anything in heaven or on the earth. In obedience to My will he named Me after the sounds the wind uttered, and he said, E-O-IH! This is now pronounced Jehovih and is written thus:*

Jehovih, the Creator

By My Presence I Create - Chapter II

The Creator tells God that it is time to teach humanity how the spiritual worlds operate and our relationship to them:

> *Jehovih said: "By virtue of My presence I created the seen and the unseen worlds.*

Creator is the very fabric of creation, not an entity that stands apart from its creation. Like quantum particles of light, the Creator is omnipresent.

By the presence of the divine, Man is inspired to language.

> *And I commanded Man to name them; and Man named the seen worlds Corpor, and the unseen worlds Es; and the inhabitants of Es he called sometimes es'eans, sometimes spirits and sometimes angels."*

The phrase "I commanded Man" raises questions about what kind of a presence would command us to do something. Perhaps we need to look at the meaning of command in a different way. By virtue of the presence of Jehovih, all things exist and move, grow, and change. The Creator is not like a man in the sky commanding the clouds to move or the planets to spin. It is an innate and intimate presence that orchestrates, inspires and moves all life. By its presence it is everything. By its presence it commands everything.

The following quote offers an interesting perspective about death. We were given physical life to learn about physicality, and we were also given death as a *gift* to allow us freedom from the burdens and limitations of physical existence. As we outgrow the physical world, we move into the spiritual worlds. This life and the next are necessary, natural steps in our evolution that bring us to another level of understanding in which we can live within the greater worlds of the infinite universe:

A corporeal body I gave to him that he might learn corporeal things, and I made death that he might raise in the firmament and inherit My etherean worlds.

Three Kinds of Worlds – Corpor, Atmospherea and Etherea

Corpor, Atmospherea and Etherea are the three kinds of worlds that exist throughout all Universes. Corpor is the physical world we as mortals on earth live within. The heavens of earth are called *atmospherea*. Atmospherea is divided into three main levels of density or dimensions, known as the *first, second and third resurrections*. The word "resurrection" simply means to rise from the dead. We cannot live in the spiritual realms unless we pass through death. Then we find that we are resurrected, for we are alive in spirit form and death was only a doorway into the next world.

Es (the unseen, spirit) I divided into two parts, and I commanded Man to name them; and he named one etherea and the other atmospherea.

These are the three kinds of worlds I created (the earth, atmospherea and etherea), but I gave different densities to the atmospherean worlds and different densities to the etherean worlds.

Etherea

The space beyond atmospherea and the earth's vortex is called *etherea*. It is composed of the space between the celestial spheres and is the most rarified and potent of all space

The densities or dimensions of Etherea are divided by forms and gateways, and arches of time and space.

Etherea is composed of a substance called *ethe,* which is the most rarified of all substance, and therefore the most powerful. Ethe exists within all things and in the midst of all dimensions. In its densest form, ethe is in physical matter. This may be the quantum particles that new science is talking about. Ethe becomes more rarified through the levels of atmospherea and into etherea. And yet, non-physical ethe exists in the midst of the physical worlds. Sentient life exists within all levels of life, from corporal to etherean:

> *For the substance of My etherean worlds I created ethe, the MOST RARIFIED. Out of ethe I made them. And I made ethe the most subtle of all created things, and gave to it power and place, not only by itself, but also power to penetrate and exist within all things, even in the midst of the corporeal worlds. And to ethe I gave dominion over both atmospherea and corpor.*

The etherean worlds are created very differently from the corporal and atmospherean worlds:

> *In the All Highest places I created the etherean worlds, and I fashioned them of all shapes and sizes, similar to My corporeal worlds. But I made the etherean worlds inhabitable within and without, with entrances and exits, in arches and curves, thousands of miles high and wide, and I overruled them with PERFECT mechanism, and in colors and movable chasms and mountains in endless change and brilliancy.*

Perhaps the entrances and exits and arches and curves of the etherean worlds are similar to wormholes, warps, and dimensional doorways.

Etherea is inhabited by beings that have passed through mortality and then the atmospherean heavens of the planet to which they were born. Ethereans live within the space between the celestial spheres.

There are many theories about the new earth and the reasons for the current weather changes and earth changes. Some of these theories have to do with the earth changing its dimension and moving into a higher dimension. This next quote could explain how the spiritual worlds of atmospherean are designed to go through dimensional changes, possibly dissolving the level closest to the earth, and allowing the earth to raise its vibration and move into another dimension:

> *Atmospherean worlds I also created in the firmament, and I gave them places and orbits and courses for themselves. But atmospherean worlds I created shapeless and void of fixed form, for they are in process of condensation or dissolution, being intermediate in condition between My etherean and My corporeal worlds.*

Atmospherea

The atmospherean worlds are much the same as the corporeal earth, having bodies of water and bodies of land and being made up of the same substance as the earth, but more rarified. This makes the transition from the earth life to the spiritual worlds easier and very familiar, but of a density that matches the density of our spiritual bodies. When we die we move into a new classroom of life that looks familiar but is much expanded to allow for our continued evolution.

Atmospherea is composed of three levels of densities or frequencies. These are called A'ji, Ji'ay, and Nebulae. They could be referred to as the *fourth, fifth,* and *sixth dimensions*:

> *Of three degrees of density I created them and I commanded Man to name them, and one he called A'ji, one Ji'ay, and one Nebulae. But all of them are composed of the same substances, being like the earth, but rarified.*

A'ji is the closest to the earth and the densest of atmospherean substance. Ji'ay is the next higher density and Nebulae is the highest.

There are many levels of density within these three divisions of atmospherea, and they are divided into plateaus, or heavens, of atmospherea. Within the first resurrection in the a'ji density are hundreds of plateaus, each one containing different types of people at different levels of evolution. "In my father's house there are many mansions." The same is true for the higher levels of ji'ay and nebulae. Every inhabited planet is surrounded by atmospherean heavens like the ones around the earth.

Vortexia - Chapter III

The order of density and dominion of life appears to operate in concentric circles moving from dense physical to the most rarified. Ether is the most ratified being able to influence and interact with the densest. The concentricity of life allows for this exchange. The earth or corpor exists within atmospherea and etherea. Atmospherea exists within etherea and includes corpor. The earth exists within the solar system. The solar system exists within the galaxy and on it goes in concentric circles infinitely.

It is vortexia that holds the celestial bodies in form, the solar system in its form, the galaxies in their form and on it goes worlds within worlds with worlds. Vortices are used to create the planets and the celestial bodies. Vortices can be any size, from the energy around an atom, or a person, to the vortex of our galaxy and beyond. When a vortex is created, it forces together the elements that exist in ethe:

> The whirlwind I made as a sign to Man of the manner of My created worlds. As you behold the power of the whirlwind gathering up the dust of the earth and driving it together, know that even so do I bring together the a'ji and ji'ay and nebulae in the firmament of heaven, and by the power of the whirlwind I create the corporeal suns and moons and stars.

And I commanded Man to name the whirlwinds in the etherean firmament and he named them vortices and wark; according to their shape he named them.

By the power of rotation, swift driving forth in the extreme parts, I condense the atmospherean worlds that float in the firmament; and these become My corporeal worlds.

In the midst of the vortices I made them, and by the power of the vortices I turn them on their axes, and carry them in the orbits I allotted to them. Wider than to the moons of a planet have I created the vortices, and they carry the moons also.

Around about some of My corporeal worlds I have given nebulous belts and rings, that Man might comprehend the rotation of My vortexian worlds.

For each and every corporeal world I created a vortex first, and by its rotation and by the places in the firmament where it travels, I caused the vortex to conceive a corporeal world.

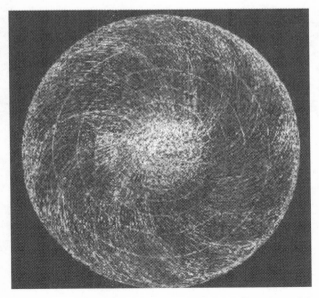

The Earth in Its Vortex with Corresponding Densities

The swirling power of the vortex causes the suns and planets to spin. The sun's vortex includes the planets of our solar system and causes the planets to rotate around the sun. Vortexia causes the atoms to spin, and holds protons and neutrons in place, just like the planets in our solar system—worlds within worlds, all divine:

A great vortex I created for the sun, and, within this vortex and subject to it, I made the vortices of many of the corporeal worlds. The sun's vortex I caused to rotate, and I gave it power to carry other vortices within it. According to their density and position are they thus carried forth and around about the sun.

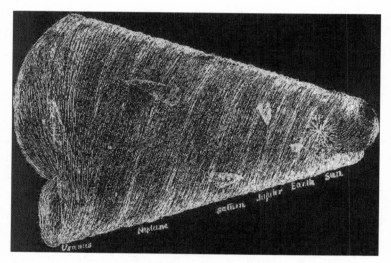

Our Solar System in Its Vortex

The Edge of the Sun's Vortex, the heliopause:

"The dimensions of the solar system are specified in terms of the mean distance from Earth to the Sun, called the astronomical unit (AU). One AU is 150 million km (about 93 million mi). Estimates for the boundary where the Sun's magnetic field ends and interstellar space begins—called the heliopause—range from 86 to 100 AU from the Sun." Microsoft ® Encarta ® 2008. © 1993-2007 Microsoft Corporation. All rights reserved.

Three States of Existence

There are three states of existence for mankind as there are the three worlds of corpor, atmospherea and etherea. The first is mortal or corporeal, which is our life on earth. Then we die and our physical form dissolves. Our spiritual body continues to exist in the atmospherean worlds around the earth. When we have matured in spirit to selfless service to all life our spiritual bodies become more rarified and we leave the earth and her heavens to live in the etherean worlds:

> *Think not, O Man, that I created the sky a barren waste, and void of use. Even as Man in the corporeal form is adapted to the corporeal earth, so is he in the spiritual form adapted to My etherean worlds. Three great estates I have bestowed on Man: the corporeal, the atmospherean and the etherean.*

If the worlds around us are divided and determined by density, then the degree of our density at the time of death will decide where we will live in the next world. Not only where we will live, but where we *can* live for we cannot exist within a dimension that is not in harmony with the state of our consciousness. Many of the books on life after death talk about going into the light—intense, bright light—and having glimpses of other worlds, where the light is so bright that a mortal visitor cannot go there unless they are protected from its intensity.

The sorting of one's spirit at death is not so much about determining if the individual has been "good" or "bad," as it is about going to a plateau where we can live according to the evolution of our consciousness. Our spirit can only live within the dimensional density for which our consciousness has prepared us. As we live on earth we are developing our spirit every day. Who we become on earth will be who we are when we move into spirit. As we evolve in spirit we move through the levels of atmospherea and then into etherea.

There is no eternal damnation only eternal evolution. There are hells and heavens around our earth, and none of them last forever. They are habitats for our evolution and they come and go according to the needs of the souls of atmospherea.

In order to prepare ourselves on earth for the next phase of our existence, which is in the spiritual worlds, we have to let go of the things that hold us down, literally. If we are really attached to the house or the car or the jewelry, then we could end up being just another ghost on the block, hanging on to our things until we learn to let go.

So what can we take with us when we die? Not anything from the physical world. We take our essence and our desires, our dreams, our fears, our anger, our grief, our joy, and our love. This is about graduating from earthly life to spiritual life, and going to the next class that is best suited for us, as we continue on to higher and higher levels of existence. We are all gods or goddesses in the making, and our evolution is infinite. We can never fail because we are immortal beings and our evolution is eternal. Eventually, everyone will develop into his or her highest potential.

The Unseen Rules the Seen - Chapter IV

The spiritual worlds and the unseen elements are the ruling forces of life. The Creator explains more about creating worlds with the etheric elements of a'ji, ji'ay, and nebulae. When we look at nature as "God's book," the visible expression of Divine Presence, we can see that there are many clues to the workings of life in its expression of beauty and the perfection of form:

> *The clouds in the air I bring into view suddenly; by different currents of wind I make the unseen visible and tangible to Man's senses. In like manner do I cause etherean currents to bring forth a'ji, and ji'ay, and nebulae, prior to making corporeal worlds.*

The interplay of the seen and the unseen is constant in our own lives and in the infinite life of the universe. Form moves and shifts and passes away from the physical world, but the spiritual part of Man and the etheric substance of the subtle realms are eternal:

> *In all the universe I have made the unseen to rule over the seen. Things that Man sees I created with a beginning and an end; but the unseen I made of endless duration. The corporeal Man I made belonging to the seen; but the spiritual Man I make as one within the unseen, and everlasting.*

When we die and leave the physical world, we gravitate to the level or plateau in atmospherea that is most in harmony with who we have become while on earth:

> *According to the condition of these different plateaus in atmospherea, whether they are near the earth or high above, so will the spirit of Man take its place in the first heaven; according to his diet and desires and behavior so will he dwell in spirit on the plateau to which he has adapted himself during his earth life.*

Our life in the spiritual worlds begins where we left off on earth. We cannot escape who we are, nor should we. All the things that we go through on earth contribute to our wisdom as we evolve in the heavens.

Just as human beings have a life cycle of birth, maturity, old age, and death, so do the planets. All planets that nurture sentient human life go through the same evolutionary periods in their development:

> *There is a time of childhood, a time of genesis, a time of old age, and a time of death to all mankind. Even so it is with all the corporeal worlds I have created. First as vapor the vortex carries it forth, and as it condenses, its friction engenders heat, and it is molten, becoming as a globe of fire in heaven. Then it takes its place as a newborn world, and I set it in the orbit prepared for it.*

In the next age, I bring it into se'mu, for it is ripe for the bringing forth of living creatures; and I bestow the vegetable and animal kingdom. Next it enters ho'tu, for it is past the age of begetting, even as the living who are in dotage. Next it enters a'du, and nothing can generate upon it. Then comes uz, and it is spirited away into unseen realms. Thus I create and dissipate planets, suns, moons, and stars.

Life works through all form, seen and unseen, as it unfolds itself. Everything in life is unique, every creature, every plant, every mountain, and every galaxy. Within all this diversity, the Creator reminds us that all the pieces of existence are parts of Him, and the truth of Him is the Unity of the whole:

Nevertheless, O Man, the seen and the unseen are but parts of My person; I am the Unity of the whole.

The Beginning of Life on Earth – Chapter V

How did life come to the earth? Jehovih explains about *se'mu*, the base substance of all life on earth, and how se'mu was the first living substance. Se'mu can be likened to jellyfish and green scum, but it is not exactly the same. The remains of se'mu have existed throughout the evolution of this world to help us learn about the workings of creation:

Let a sign be given to Man that he may comprehend se'mu. Thereupon Jehovih caused the jellyfish and the green scum of water to be permanently coming forth in all ages, that Man might understand the Age of Se'mu, when the earth and the shores by the water, and the waters also, were covered over with commingled atmosphere and corporeal substance.

How can such diverse life forms emerge from one substance, se'mu? The diversity of life upon the earth was created by the location of the se'mu and the variances of light upon it:

> *According to their respective places and the light upon se'mu, so I quickened them in their color, adapted to their dwelling places.*

In My Likeness

Some people have interpreted the statement of Man being made in God's likeness to mean that we look like the Creator. Here, the phrase "in my likeness" means that Man has similar traits to the Creator. The word "Creator" describes the essence of all that is, seen and unseen. Creator is not an individual person, but all life everywhere:

> *Jehovih said: Because of My presence, I quickened into life all that lives, or ever has lived. Because I am male and female, even in My likeness, thus I made them. Because I am the power to quicken into life, so in likeness of Me I made them with the power to bring forth.*

All life is constantly new and individual throughout creation:

> *Each and every living thing I created new upon the earth, of a kind each to itself, and I created not one living thing out of another.*

I Am Life Itself

Here is another deeper statement of the Creator's person and the relationship of all life to the Creator. It is a statement of the eternal, the infinite, and the intimate reality of Divine Presence:

> *Such is My person and My spirit, being from everlasting to everlasting; and when I bring a new world into the time of se'mu, lo and behold, My presence quickens the substance into life. According to the locality*

31

and the surroundings, so do I bring forth the different species, for they are flesh of My flesh and spirit of My spirit. To them I give themselves; nevertheless, they are all members of My Person.

All that lives is the body and spirit of the Creator. All that lives is a part of the Creator. Life itself is the Creator.

Here is the answer to an ancient question: Which came first, the chicken or the egg?

Without seed I created the life that is in them.

How is that possible? Perhaps with the understanding of vortexia, one could speculate that it could be possible to drive the elements into form and then breathe divine life into them:

Behold, I make a whirlwind in etherea, hundreds and hundreds of millions of miles across, and it drives to the center a corporeal world from that which was unseen. I blow my breath upon the planet, and lo, Man comes forth, inquiring: "Who am I, and what is my destiny?" Book of Ben, Chapter II

The First Man - Chapter VI

Now Man appears on the scene. The first men like beings were called the A'su, meaning Adam. They were human like, but not yet immortal. They began to ask the great question, 'Who am I?'

Hear me, O Man; I will clear up the mysteries of heaven and earth and before your judgment. You are the highest, and come to the greatest of all kingdoms; from Great Jehovih will you learn wisdom, and none will oppose you.

A'su was shown the elements of life in their different places within the worlds of spirit and matter:

> Behold, O Man! As a farmer sows corn in one place, and wheat in another, and roots in another, and flax—everything in a separate place; even so does Jehovih store the ingredients of which worlds are made—everything to its place—the substance of the iron in one place, the substance of the stones in another, the substance of the vegetable kingdom in another, and even so of the substance of the animal kingdom; and the oils and sand; for He has places in the firmament of heaven for all of them.

> These that you saw are the a'ji and ji'ay and the nebulae; and amidst them in places there is se'mu also. Let no one say: Yonder is hydrogen only and yonder oxygen only. The divisions of the substances of His creations are not as Man would make them. All the elements are to be found not only in places near at hand, but in distant places also.

The evolution of the earth is not a random unfoldment of life, but an orchestrated series of events that create the rich and abundant world we live on. It is obvious that Creator knew we would need coal and oil and gas for our evolution. Now the question is where we go from here when we have used up these resources and how do we clean up the mess we made in the process?

> When the Father drives forth His worlds in the heavens, they gather a sufficiency of all things. So it happens that when a corporeal world is yet new and young it is carried forth, not by random, but purposely, in the regions suited to it. Hence there is a time of se'mu, a time for falling nebulae, to bury deep the forests and se'muan beds, to provide coal and manure for a time thereafter.

> So is there a time when the earth passes a region in the firmament when sand and oil are rained upon it and covered up, and gases bound and sealed up for the coming generations of Man.

Then Man arrives on the scene and the angels come to help them:

> *Out of se'mu I made Man, and Man was but as a tree, but dwelling in ha'k (darkness); and I called him A'su. (Adam) I looked over the wide heavens that I had made, and I saw countless millions of spirits of the dead, that had lived and died on other corporeal worlds before the earth was made.*

At this stage, A'su was as a tree, being unaware of his own species. He was so dumb he did not know he was different from the other animals around him. In answer to the call of the Great Spirit, millions of angels from other worlds came to help uplift A'su. They were angels who died in infancy or before birth and had not had a full earth life. These angels came to our world to help with the beginnings of Man on the earth. They came to learn what it is like to be mortal and to experience the beginning of a new world.

Some theories of humanity's origin include the idea that *alien* beings from other worlds "created" us and have nurtured us since our beginning. These theories are based on ancient records that talk of beings from beyond who interacted with Man and who have returned at different times to guide humanity's evolution. It is interesting how similar these ideas are to this text. It is also interesting that the alien theories do not seem to include the possibility that these beings were angelic beings from other worlds instead of mortal beings from outer space:

> *I spoke in the firmament, and My voice reached to the uttermost places. And there came in answer to the sounds of My voice, myriads of angels from the roadway in heaven, where the earth traveled. I said to them, "Behold! I have created a new world; come and enjoy it. You will learn from it how it was with other worlds in ages past.*

Adam's Rib

The story of Adam's rib is slightly different in *the Oahspe*. Remember, we are not talking about a single person as Adam, we are talking about the first race of human-like beings in their beginning stages before the angels companioned them. The angels took on mortal form *by* the side of the A'su or Adam and not *from* the side of the Adam:

> *And now the earth was in the latter days of se'mu, and the angels could readily take on corporeal bodies for themselves; out of the elements of the earth they clothed themselves, by force of their wills, with flesh and bones.*
>
> *By the side of the A'suans they took on corporeal forms. And I said, go and deliver A'su from darkness, for he will also rise in spirit to inherit My etherean worlds.*

The word for spirit is Es. The stories of creation have been handed down through generations, and could have easily been changed to from Es to Eve. By the side of Adam, the angels, or Es'eans, took on mortal form.

The angels watched over the A'su, day and night. The Creator warned them not to cohabitate with the A'su, or they would become bound to the lower heavens by their love for their offspring:

> *Go forth and partake of all that is on the earth; but partake not of the tree of life, lest in that labor you become procreators and as if dead to the heavens from where you came.*

The angels would not be able to rise above the lower heavens until their offspring of seven generations had been uplifted. This is still the law of responsibility for one's children in the heavens.

The Immortal Man

A new species called *Man* came into being, for the angels did partake of the tree of life, and approximately seventy-two thousand years ago the union of mortals and angels created the new race of Man:

> *And there was born of the first race (A'su/Adam) a new race called Man, and Jehovih took the earth out of the travail of se'mu, and the angels gave up their corporeal bodies.*

Far out! Yes it is, but it may be true. This could explain the missing link between apes and Man and how Man became an immortal being. It was probably not an accident that the angels cohabitated with Man. This is the way of all worlds that grow human beings. It was not a sin to cohabitate with the A'su/ Adam. The warning from Creator was to let the angels know that there would be great consequence from partaking of the tree of life that would bind them to the lower worlds for many years. The angels would indeed fall from their higher heavens and would be bound in the lower heavens by their love and responsibility to their offspring.

The new race of Man was not thrown out of the Garden for cohabitating with the angels, we are all still in the Garden. Perhaps Man felt like he was closed out of the Garden because he could no longer be with the angelic ones.

When the angels gave up their corporal forms, they became the guardians of Man. The earth was new and there were no heavens or guiding angels for the earth. As the humans of the new race died, the spiritual worlds began to be populated. The angels who helped to create Man had to organize the heavens in preparation for receiving the spirits of their children, the now immortal Man of the earth.

Once the seed of immortality had been planted in Man, the Creator promises that the immortal seed will not be lost, and that mankind will continue to carry the immortal seed until this planet goes into dissolution:

As I have quickened the seed of the firstborn, so
will I quicken all seed to the end of the earth.

Reincarnation

Jehovih makes a clear statement about the ability of a person to be born again into a human body. The doctrine or theory of *reincarnation* has become very popular, but that does not mean it is a universal reality:

And each and every man-child and woman-child
born into life will I quicken with a new spirit,
which will proceed out of Me at the time of conception. Neither
will I give to any spirit of the higher or lower heaven
power to enter a womb, or a fetus of a womb,
and be born again.

So what is all the literature describing reincarnation about? If it is physically impossible to come back into a physical body after we have died, then how could the concept of reincarnation work? The earthbound spirits possess people and impose their memory of their lives upon them. These spirits often possess small children and raise them believing in reincarnation. They also come through mediums and offer information about a person's 'past life'. Sometimes, they influence a person to experience the life of a specific spirit when it was alive, and in this way convince the mortal person that the life of that spirit was their own. We are meant to learn how to discern the truth from any spirit that manifests to us:

For a season, your God has suffered this also to come to pass—that the
spirits say there is no God; that there is no higher heaven than to dwell

upon the earth, to enjoy the earthly things; to be reincarnated, and to live over and over in mortality.

O Man, beware of spirits who say…Resurrection comes by reincarnation—first a stone, then lead, then silver, then gold, then a tree, then a worm, then an animal, and then Man, or that a spirit re-enters the womb and is born again in mortality. The Book of Discipline Chapter III

Etherean Lights -Chapter VII

As there are seasons on the earth, so are there seasons or cycles through which our solar system passes as its travels around the galaxy. These cycles were created to assist in the evolution of life on planets such as the earth. There are cycles of darkness and cycles of light, and places in between. The cycles of light are called *dan'ha,* and they were created to remind Man of the spiritual worlds and inspire Man to new inventions and better ways of living:

> *Jehovih said: Let a sign be given to the inhabitants of the earth that they may comprehend dan'ha in the firmament of heaven. For even as I bequeath to the earth a time for creating the living, and a time for angels to come and partake of the first fruits of mortality and immortality, so will Man at certain times and seasons receive testimony from My hosts in heaven.*

As the earth travels through the galaxy we enter areas, or bands of light called *etherean lights.* Our solar system enters these bands every three thousand years. They bring a tremendous increase of light to our solar system. This increase in light has a quickening effect on the evolution of all life.

When the earth enters the etherean lights, the spiritual dimensions of the planet change as the density of our atmosphere lessens. The increased light, which creates a more rarified atmosphere, makes it possible for the angels of the higher heavens to visit the earth because the lower atmospherean heavens become less dense:

> *And Jehovih caused the earth, and the family of the sun to travel in an orbit, the circuit of which required of them four million seven hundred thousand years. And he placed in the line of the orbit, at distances of 3,000 years, etherean lights, which as the earth passes through, angels from the second heaven come into its corporeal presence.*

The orbit of our solar system is 4.7 million years according to this text. It does not say if this is the orbit around our galaxy. The *Encyclopedia of Science Heavens 2* says that our solar system rotates around the galactic sun every 225 million years. Perhaps *the Oahspe* is talking about a different orbit, or perhaps not.

There has been a lot of talk about the photon, or Manasic field of light during the last twenty years. It could be the same thing as the etherean lights, except that most writings say that the earth enters the photon field approximately every twelve thousand years. The Oahspe says we enter the etherean lights every three thousand years. If these are indeed two different light fields that our solar system travels through, it would be interesting to contemplate what might happen when our solar system enters both at the same time.

As our solar system travels through the galaxy, it takes a serpentine path, winding its way through the areas of increased light and lesser light. The fields of lesser light within our galaxy create an atmosphere in which the Beast rises within humanity and the progress of light on earth often falls toward darkness. Just as we experience day and night, the solar system has times of light and of darkness.

> *The length of the great serpent is approximately 1,500 million miles long. The numbers of the beast shall be sixty-six, and six hundred and*

sixty-six, and the parts thereof. Because in the coil of the cycle, behold the distances are two-thirds of a circle, whether it be a hundred or a thousand, or three times a thousand. Jehovih rolleth up the heavens and braideth the serpents of the firmament into His cyclic coil. He is the circle without beginning or end. The Oahspe, Book of Fragapatti, Chapter XVII.

Angels on Earth

When a world moves into the etherean lights, the higher angels can come into corporeal presence, they come to the earth. Do they take on mortal form? Do they work through subtle presence? There are many stories of people whose lives have been saved or helped by the sudden presence of a stranger and then their disappearance. They turn to thank the stranger and there is no one there. It would seem easier for the angels to work through the subtle to inspire and assist and only take on physical form in emergencies. Oahpse does not make it clear as to whether the angels take on physical form throughout their stay on the earth.

The dispensation of visitations and assistance from the higher angels happens only at the beginning of the etherean lights and lasts approximately two hundred years. The 1850's was the beginning of the etherean lights. Look at the leap of evolution that has happened since then. We have had a great burst of light, knowledge, inventions and assistance.

Some people give credit to the ET's for our accelerated evolution. Perhaps there are mortal beings from other worlds visiting this world and influencing us. Perhaps both ET's and angelics are here. It would seem that the angelic worlds are the most common visitors, for our ancestors have much at stake and the ruling angelics of our galaxy would hold much more power and knowledge than any mortal from another world. Perhaps we sometimes mistake angelics for ET's and vice versa.

During the times of the etherean lights the spirits of the newly dead are able to interact openly with mortals. Why? So that humanity can know of a fact of the existence of life after death and learn about the spiritual worlds:

> *And Jehovih gave this sign to Man on earth: in the beginning of the light of dan'ha, the spirits of the newly dead will have power to take upon themselves the semblance of corporeal bodies, and appear and talk face to face with mortals. Every 3,000 years, Jehovih gave this sign on earth, that those who learned the powers and capacities of such familiar spirits might bear testimony in regard to the origin of Man on earth.*

In the late 1800's many writings were published about the spiritual worlds and about the spiritual essence of humanity. Spiritualism became an organized body of knowledge to bear witness to the existence of the spiritual realms. Mediumship became common place and to this day is growing in acceptance. In the past the different forms of Shamanism were used to communicate with the spiritual worlds and only the trained ones could do this work as a general rule. Now the gates of heaven are open and all people can experience the presence of the spiritual dimensions, if they chose.

When the earth passes through the etherean lights, the old ways are often set aside, new inventions spring up everywhere, and the people of the earth are inspired to change and to a more spiritual way of living:

> *Let him who will become wise, enumerate the great lights of My serpent; for in such times I set aside things that are old and establish My chosen anew.*

A reminder here: "My chosen" refers to the people who choose to embrace the Creator for it is in choosing that we are chosen.

The etherean lights herald times of great change. People, organizations, and governments that are hanging onto old ways of being that are no longer appropriate will have the most difficulty during the times of the etherean light. This is the time when the Creator declares that we must move forward in ways that are in harmony with the positive evolution of our world.

The times of lesser light influence humanity to become more interested in the physical, tangible things of this earth and less interested in spiritual matters. Man tends toward a more self-centered existence, the Beast rises and war is often the result. The times of increased light—as we are now moving into—inspire Man to new inventions and new discoveries. People no longer tolerate injustices and corruption in the church or the state. There is a thirst for a more spiritual life and a life of purpose.

We are at the beginning of a new three thousand-year cycle that begins the *Kosmon Era*. The kosmon era is a special time in the evolution of every planet such as the earth, when we stop fighting with each other and embrace world peace.

We are to achieve a permanent end to war on earth during the age of kosmon.

So, why are we having so much unrest around the world? As the light increases, the shadows become more obvious and all our wrongs rise up to meet us. The inequities and injustices are coming into the light to be seen and changed. The conflicts and prejudices held within the races of our world are coming to a head. The earth will no longer tolerate the hatred, the killing, and the struggles for control and power. Governments that hang onto unjust governance will not survive. The coming of the light will require change. We will have to let go of that which cannot exist in the new light of the Creator.

The Higher Angels

When the angels of the second resurrection in atmospherea come to the earth, they do not come as individuals, nor do they come to a single individual. Classically, they come as a "voice," a light, and sometimes as a beautiful fragrance:

As ambassadors they come, in companies of hundreds and thousands and tens of thousands, and these are called the etherean hosts of the Most High. They come not as single individuals; they come not for a single individual mortal.

Why don't the higher angels come as individuals? The higher angels only work in groups and for the greater good of the greatest number of beings. They find strength together and are able to do far greater works together than as an individual. They do not live from an egocentric perspective. They seek the good of the whole. Just as they do not come as individuals, so they do not come for a single individual. They come to people who are working in groups for the greater good of all. They help those who help others. They come for all of humanity. They do not give their names for they come in groups and not as individuals.

The earthbound angels and the angels of lower atmospherea, or the first resurrection, come as individuals to individuals. They often seek family members and friends. Their evolution is still singular in purpose. Whether they want to relate to someone they love or harass people for their entertainment, they are bound by the limitations of their consciousness. It is common for them to use a name to identify themselves.

The individual presence of an angel is usually a declaration that they are earthbound souls. An elder brother or sister in the next dimension can have helpful information for us, but they are by no means high-raised angels. They may want to help, but just as in earth life they have their own point of view. Remember that a communication from any being, mortal or discarnate is not binding upon us. We are to judge for ourselves what information we will embrace.

> *What comes to you from a man is indirect inspiration; what comes from an angel is indirect; and what comes from the Gods is indirect.*
> *Chapter IX, Book of Inspiration*

The Heavens

The heavens of the first resurrection span from the earth to approximately two thousand miles above the earth. Beyond the first resurrection are the higher heavens of the second and third resurrection, which extends to approximately three thousand miles above the earth to the edge of the earth's vortex, called the *Bridge of Chinvat*. Within these heavens are many plateaus where the spirits of once mortals live. The majority of plateaus are closest to the earth because the majority of spirits are closest to the earth.

With the appearance of Man on earth there came a need for the creation of the heavens to receive the immortal souls of the new race when they die. The earth and its heavens were new and its infrastructure had to be created. This work fell to the angels who cohabitated with the A'su and were bound to their offspring for six generations. We are also responsible to our offspring for six generations. This bondage is one of love and of responsibility:

> *Behold, you now have sons and daughters on the earth; by your love to them you are bound spirits of the lower heaven. Until you redeem them in wisdom and power even to the sixth generation you will not again arise and inherit My emancipated heavens.*

What does it mean to redeem our children? We are responsible to help uplift them above their selfish perspectives. By our examples and by our love and understanding we can inspire our children. Then we are responsible in the heavens to raise them up in spirit and help them to grow out of the lower heavens and into the higher heavens, where they can contribute to life in love and selfless service. Of course, we must be growing in that direction as well.

Spiritual ignorance has caused the heavens of the earth to become a fouling nest of ignorant souls. This creates an atmosphere where people do not understand their responsibilities or even care to help each other. When the earth and the lower heavens become filled with ignorant lower spirits, it is time for the earth to change, because this state of ignorance plays back upon the earth and creates more of the same consciousness. It is often the children who suffer, because they are so vulnerable to subtle influences.

The responsibility of our ancestors to inspire us is not over until we have learned to inspire others and ourselves.

The more we inspire our children while we and they are on the earth, the easier will be our own transition into spirit and the less we will be bound to the earth.

The angels who uplifted the A'su were given the task of organizing the heavens above the earth in preparation for those who would pass into spirit. The angels had to learn how to do these things as it is done on other worlds. What other worlds? Some scientists are beginning to speculate that there are thousands and thousands of habitable planets around many of the suns. There are a multitude of other planets throughout the galaxies like ours that are growing immortal beings.

Etherean Chiefs and Chieftess

Just as the angels of the A'su were responsible to organize the heavens, so are the ethereans responsible to govern the etherean worlds and the inhabited planets in every galaxy. These beings are called *Chiefs or Chieftess*. There are also ethereans who are Gods and Goddesses from many other worlds who work with the Chiefs and Chieftess, and beings who are just ethereans from other worlds. At the beginning of establishing the heavens for the earth the Creator sent an etherean Chief to teach the angels how to organize the heavens:

> *And I will allot to you a Chief, who is wise in experience in founding heavenly kingdoms; and he (or she) will appoint, from among you, officers, and messengers and ashars, and asaphs, and es'enaurs, and you will be numbered and apportioned in your labor and places, like My other lower heavens on other worlds.*

The earth and the heavens of the earth are womb-like containers for the cultivation of the soul of Man. We stay within the earth's heavens until we reach the point of evolution in which we are in complete service to all life. Then we are free to live and serve in the infinite space of the etherean worlds, forever.

We are born into a physical form and the earth is our home. Here, we learn the laws of cause and effect, and gain a sense of who we are. Then we are born into the world of spirit. The heavens become our home and we grow into a deeper understanding of who we are. We then evolve beyond the heavens of the earth and into the infinite space of the etherean worlds to continue our evolution, forever. In a sense we are born into mortality and born again into spirit and then born again into infinite etherea.

Gods and Goddesses

Within the organization of the spiritual worlds of the earth there is a hierarchy of responsibility. The leaders of the angels are called *God* or *Goddess*. The angels who assist God are called "Lords" and "Lord Gods," and they have specific tasks within the heavens or in regards to mortals. Mankind learned to call God Lord *and Lord God* when the false gods took control of the oracles and temples thousands of years ago.

To each God or Goddess there is a season of service. The lengths of these seasons vary, but they all fall within a cycle of three thousand years. There could be several changes of Gods of our earth within a three thousand-year cycle. With the end of each season, the different Gods graduate from this world to etherea. When the former God or Goddess leaves the heavens of the earth, a new angel who once lived on the earth is placed in charge as the new God or Goddess of the earth:

> *And God and his Lords will have dominion from two hundred years to a thousand or more years; but never more than 3,000 years. According to the regions of dan (light) into which I bring the earth, so will be the terms of the office of My Gods and My Lords.*

When it is time for a God to leave the earth, the angels of the higher heavens go with the God or Goddess into etherea. The ethereans come in ships of light to escort the angels of the earth to etherea. The ethereans are angels sent by the Creator to assist in the graduation of the angels of the higher heavens of the earth. The angels who are prepared to leave the earth's atmosphere are called *brides and bridegrooms of the Creator*. This event is a great graduation party for millions of the souls of Man. These angels have reached a level of consciousness wherein they have become truly enlightened. It is interesting to note that life does not allow the angels to "escape" from this world and its heavens before they have evolved into beings who are truly an asset to the universe:

47

*At the termination of the dominion of My God and his Lords they
will gather together in these My bound heavens (atmospherea), all such
angels as have been prepared in wisdom and strength for resurrection
to My etherean kingdoms. And these angels will be called Brides and
Bridegrooms to the Creator, for they are Mine and in My service.*

Etherean Ships

Groups of etherean angels travel to earth in huge ships of light during
the times of harvest. These etherean ships are built to hold all the angels
that are leaving the earth for etherea, being hundreds of thousands
and sometimes millions of souls. These are not UFO crafts. They are
ships made of light and sound. They are *etherean ships* and the physical
eye cannot see them, unless they lower their lights to allow mortals to
see them. They can be seen with our spiritual eyes. *The Oahspe* gives
several descriptions of how the etherean ships are built and how they
are propelled by light and consciousness. There are also descriptions of
the atmospherean ships. Remember, all the things we have created or
invented are but a small reflection of what exists in the earth's heavens
and the worlds beyond:

*And to the God and his Lords, with the Brides and Bridegrooms, I
will send down from etherea ships in the time of dan; by My etherean
Gods and Goddesses will the ships descend to these heavens and receive
God and his lords with the Brides and Bridegrooms, and carry them
up to the exalted regions I have prepared for them.*

The term "exalted regions" is a description of etherea. Etherea is of
the highest vibration for angelics and can only be inhabited by those
who have evolved to a level of consciousness that can live within this
space.

The Harvest

The cycles of growth and change in the heavens are divided into the lesser cycles of dan and the greater cycles of dan'ha:

> *And all such as ascend will be called a Harvest to Me through My God and Lords. And the time of My Harvests will be according to each dan, which is two hundred years, four hundred years, six hundred years, and five hundred years; and these will be called My lesser cycles, because they are the times of the tables of prophecy, which I give to My servants.*

Note that a servant is someone who serves another. This can be another person, a cause, an organization, or an ideal. The use of the word "servant" does not mean a slave or someone who does the bidding of another in disregard of one's freedom. We always have a choice of whom or what we will serve in this life and the next. Many people choose to serve themselves, and many choose to serve a greater cause or a noble idea. Those who choose to serve the Creator are servants of the Creator. By serving a noble cause we would be serving the Creator.

Here is a brainteaser: A dan'ha is every three thousand years. There are seven dans within each dan'ha, and approximately thirty years times six within each dan. All Harvests occur at the end of each dan:

> *I have created seven dans for each and every dan'ha; and I have given six generations of mortals to each dan.*

For those who want to pursue understanding the cycles of our planet more thoroughly, *The Oahspe* has a section in the Book of Cosmogony and Prophecy about how to discern the cycles of the evolution of the earth.

According to the ebb and flow of life within the heavens of the earth, so are the cycles of the Gods and Goddesses of this world. So also is the flow of the evolution of the angels of the heavens. That does not change when we move to the next world.

Sometimes, the higher heavens must wait for the angels to reach a point of consciousness in which they are ready to leave the heavens of the earth; and sometimes, large groupings of angels are ready quickly. The times of evolution of the angels in the heavens are ruled by the times of darkness and the times of light, just as our life on earth is ruled by the times of darkness and the times of light.

Many accounts of going across to the spiritual world and coming back, have said that the spiritual worlds are just like the earth. This is not because the angels are copying our world it is because they inspired us to make ours like theirs. Here is a description of the duties of the angels in the first resurrection.

> *As you become organic in heaven, with rulers and teachers, and physicians; and with capitals, and cities, and provinces; and with hospitals, and nurseries, and schools, and factories, even so will you ultimately inspire Man on the earth to the same things.*

The Organization of the Heavens - Chapter VIII

In esoteric teachings, there are references to the *Akashic records*. These are said to be the records of heaven. This next quote speaks of the existence of records and their purpose. Perhaps these records are the same as those referred to as the Akashic records.

The records discussed in the Oahspe contain accounts of each person's life on earth and then in the heavens. When an angel leaves the heavens of earth and goes to etherea, the Orian Chiefs or Chieftess and the Archangels of etherea (who compose the governing body of etherea) receive the angel's records. These records help the Orian Chiefs in etherea decide where best to place the incoming angels and Gods.

> *And in the times of My harvest, a copy of these records will be taken up to My etherean kingdoms and filed with My Orian Chiefs and Archangels in the roadway of travel of the great serpent, for their deliberations as to the progress and management of the inhabitants of the earth and her heavens.*

(See the end of the Book of Jehovih for a more in depth explanation of the great serpent.)

It appears that none of the universe is unorganized or random. We just can't see all the things that are happening around us all of the time. This is probably a good thing!

The organization of the heavens and etherea are not any different than they are on earth, except that the higher heavens are free of greed, fear and domination. To clarify the different types of organization:

Earth: Presidents, Vice Presidents, Secretaries, Kings and Queens, Generals, etc.

Secondary: Counsels, parliaments, senates, houses, mayors, representatives, and committees.

Atmospherea:
God and Goddesses, Lords, and Lord Gods
Secondary: High counsels and groupings of angels with various responsibilities.

Etherea:
Oe'tan, Nirvanian, Orian Chiefs, Gods and Goddesses, Archangels and Ethereans. There are holy counsels and groupings of these angels with

various responsibilities, like overseeing the evolution of stars that regulate earths and managing sections of the galaxies.

Hells

The spiritual cycles of the earth include periods of time when the lower heavens turn to chaos and destruction. During these phases of darkness, the spirits of the lower heavens become defiant and rebellious. They leave the heavens and run back to the earth, bringing chaos and suffering. During these times, the spirits of the newly dead are drawn into the chaos and suffering, and they become bound to the earth. This creates a "fouling nest" in which the darkness is self-perpetuating.

And mortals, who will be slain in war,
will be born in spirit in chaos on the battlefields;
in chaos will such spirits enter the es world.
And they will not know that they are dead (as to earth
life), but will still keep fighting right and left.

Hells are created by the deeds of mortals and angels who lose themselves in fear, selfishness, hatred, and the enjoyment of the suffering of others. Hell is not a permanent place where someone goes because they are not of a particular belief or they have not lived a perfect life. Hell is an accumulation of thousands and millions of souls who are deeply lost. These beings are attracted to each other by their way of life when they lived on earth and their state of mind. When the hells become large enough, the spirits within are trapped in the chaos of their own creation. These hells exist near the lower heavens, near the earth, and sometimes on the earth. Hells are created above the earth where there is war, and especially in places where war has been going on for a long time. These places produce feuds between people that keep becoming wars, or where governments exist that breed hatred and suffering in their people. They are very large and self-perpetuating. It is not unusual for people on earth to be inspired to evil deeds by the hells around them.

When the earth moves into the time of the etherean lights, the ethereans and the higher angels of the earth work together to break up the hells and retrieve the souls that are lost in madness. During these times, the angels prepare places in the heavens to take these souls to what we might call "hospitals" to help revive them and teach them of a higher way of life:

> *The enemy will take them, in these heavens, and cast them in the places of torment, which they will have built, and they will not know peace or wisdom. And the work of your heavens will become as nothing. And you will turn to going about delivering hells and the spirits in chaos.*

It is important that the anchor on earth—which is the place feeding the hell—be broken or changed in order to stop the creation of another hell. Burning down a city, sinking continents, changing poles, or large earthquakes, volcanoes and hurricanes have been used to accomplish the breaking of the anchors of hells.

We are certainly having our share of earthquakes, tsunamis, and strange weather patterns, collapses of governments and destruction of cities from anarchy. It is interesting that many of the earth changes and changing of governments are happening in areas where there have been many wars, starvation, and abuse of humanity that would indeed create hells in the heaven.

We are in a new time on earth. We have the opportunity to change the anchors of darkness upon the earth before the angels must break the anchors to clear the heavens of the hells that have been created over the last three thousand years.

We are doing this when we refuse to embrace the destructive ways of the ruling bodies of our countries. When we clean up ghettos and educate the people to better ways of life we are changing the hells of poverty and hopelessness. We are doing this when we help those who have survived tsunamis and other earth changes and give them hope and a better way of life. We are doing this when we raise our children to embrace peace and the sacredness of all life on earth.

The Book of Jehovih ends with an introduction to the Kosmon Era and the coming of the light:

> *And when the inhabitation of the earth will be completed, and the nations will have established civil communion around from east to west, in that same time I will bring the earth into the Kosmon era, and My angel ambassadors, Gods and Goddesses, will render up the records of these heavenly kingdoms.*
>
> *Through them will I reveal to mortals the creation of My worlds, and the history and dominion of My Gods and Lords on the earth, even from this day down to the time of Kosmon.*

* * *

Levels of Atmospherea

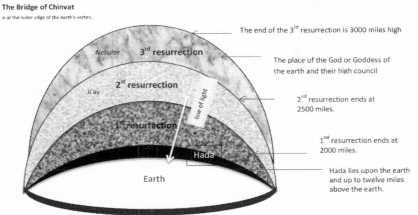

The different shades of the levels of atmospherea show the density of each one. The darkest is the densest and lowest in consciousness. The first resurrection is the most populated, then the second resurrection and the third resurrection is the least populated.

Chart of the Heavens

The illustration shown above is a diagram of the spiritual dimensions, or heavens, of the earth. The spiritual dimensions of the earth, called atmospherea, begin on the earth where the earthbound souls reside and extend approximately three thousand miles above the earth, near the outer limits of the earth's vortex at the bridge of Chinvat. Atmospherea is divided into three sections: the first, second and third resurrections:

> *Around about My corporeal worlds I placed atmospherea; for, as the earth and other corporeal worlds provide a womb for the spirit of Man, so have I made atmospherea the substance for a womb for the souls of Man.*

Hada

The first narrow, dark area of the Chart represents the spiritual planes nearest the earth and rests on the earth. It is called *Hada*. This place is at grade one and below in the levels of the spiritual worlds. It is where the spirits of the dead go when they are in a state of ignorance regarding life after death. These beings only understand the earth and the material plane. They have not developed spiritually. They wander about the earth because they are unable to move beyond it:

> *And your God weeps for you; because, in the time of your death, you will stand in heaven in grade one, even as the spirits of the beasts of the field. Your present knowledge will be void, and your vigor, only as a newborn child. And my angels who are wise and strong will take you about, in hada, the heavenly plateau that rests on the earth, and divert you with things closely related betwixt the two worlds, that you can be made to comprehend yourself and your Creator's work.*

There are many spirits who dwell on or near the earth below the first resurrection of atmospherea:

> *Of grade one, there are hundreds of millions of angels strolling about on the earth, crying out: I want to go to Brahma; I want to go to Buddha; I want to go to Jesus; and I want to go to Kriste.*

> *And I made the animal heaven to rest on the face of the lands of the earth even the same as the place of the es'yan (angels) in grade one. He that serves himself only, will stand at grade one.*

Beings below grade one are called *drujas, engrafters,* and *fetals.* They are below grade one because they are completely ignorant of anything beyond the earth. Spirits below grade one attach themselves to mortals as engrafters and fetals. When a person sees ghosts and experiences haunted places, they are seeing earthbound souls, or drujas:

> ...*such angels that know nothing more than babes, though for the most part they were full grown adults as to earth-life. Some are fetals, some engrafters (professional re-incarnators), who dwell with one mortal during his life-time, and then engraft themselves on another mortal during his life time, and so on, calling themselves re-incarnated, and in fact knowing no other heavens, being disbelievers in the All Person and in my exalted kingdoms.*
>
> *Such as are below grade one, I have classed this day as drujas, because they have not left the earth and entered the first resurrection. They inhabit mostly the oldest cities and places of filth and indecency; nevertheless, they also inhabit the palaces of kings and queens and emperors and popes and priests and rich people.*

The spirits in grade one and the druja spirits below grade one are very interactive with mortals because they live side by side in the same places. These spiritual realms are often referred to as the lower realms or the Bardos.

The First Resurrection Above Grade One

The first resurrection begins at twelve miles above the earth and ends at two thousand miles above the earth. The first resurrection has many heavens or plateaus. Each ascending plateau or heaven in atmospherea is more rarified, with increasing levels of light. In the first resurrection the spirits or angels range from above grade one up to grade fifty. Those of grade fifty are the most evolved angels in the first resurrection of atmospherea. They are fifty percent for themselves and fifty percent for others:

> *Whether on earth or in heaven, the same rules apply to both:*
> *He that serves himself one-half, and serves others one-half,*
> *will stand at grade fifty.*
> *He that serves himself three-quarters, and others one quarter,*
> *will stand at grade twenty-five.*
> *He that serves himself one-quarter, and others three-quarters, will stand at grade seventy-five.*
> *He that serves himself only, will stand at grade one.*
> *He that serves others wholly, will stand at grade ninety-nine.*
> *And whoso serves accordingly, himself or others, will stand in grade even as his works manifest.*
> *The Book of Judgment, Chapter VI*

When an individual spirit inspires a mortal, the spirit is from the first resurrection. These spirits often give their name when they come to speak with a mortal. A deceiving spirit of the first resurrection will often give a false name of someone important to influence the mortal. Angels are not necessarily wise or benevolent just because they are angels. By the merit of the message alone are we to judge whether the information is helpful to us.

This next quote explains the difference between the inspirations of the angels of the second resurrection and the angels of the first resurrection:

> *For, by the inspirations of the angels of your God [second resurrection], the individual entity of a mortal is directed in its normal growth; but by the angels of the first resurrection, mortals are used abnormally, by entrancement, by miracles, or by sar'gis, oracles, or otherwise.*
>
> *Book of Inspiration*

What does it mean to be used abnormally? The highest way to uplift a person is to inspire them to higher thoughts or actions. This allows a person to make their own decisions. The beings of the second resurrection are the guardian angels of mortals. The beings of the first resurrection come to us using ways that are more imposing of their perspective or opinion. Sometimes they will come to us just to let us know that they are fine or they miss us or they love us:

> *For the spirits, who speak through them, (those who give personal information for self's sake,) will be of the first resurrection, and know not Me nor the higher kingdoms.*
>
> *Verily they will be of the same order as the spirits who minister in the churches and temples, being such spirits as have not yet been delivered up from the earth.*

All the angels of the first resurrection are still bound to the earth in one way or another, whether to a family member or a congregation or an organization, they are bound by desire, by love, by anger and hate, by lack of fulfillment, etc. The angels of the higher heavens are no longer attached to the earth. They serve the earth, but they are not attached to individuals or religions or affiliations of the earth. Their perspective is universal.

At the time of the great flood, approximately twenty-four thousand years ago, there were many kingdoms, or heavens, in atmospherea. The first resurrection's heavens then spanned from the earth upwards for two thousand miles. The lowest of the heavens spanned from the earth to twelve miles above the earth.

The Second and Third Resurrections

Now we move to the second and third resurrections of atmospherea. In order to live in this division of the spiritual worlds, an individual must live at least fifty percent for others. The angels of the higher heavens have committed to unity and no longer work as a single unit. They only return to earth in a "line of light" with other angelics. It is important to note that they do not come for a single individual or as an individual:

> They come not as single individuals; they come not for a single individual mortal. And they covenanted themselves to Jehovih to not return again single-handed to minister to mortals; neither to return again to mortals save they came in phalanxes (a unified line of angels or a line of light), and only then when duly authorized and directed by their most Holy Council, and their chief, who was God.
>
> This rule is also uniform in all my heavenly kingdoms: After entrance into the second resurrection, none of the angels return as individuals, to commune with mortals, except as I have mentioned, or save when especially commissioned by me or my Lords.

The inorganic heavens on the earth and the first resurrection are the most populated areas of the heavens. The least populated are in the second and third resurrection:

> The least of my organic kingdoms contains half a thousand million angels; and many of them contain five thousand million.

The third resurrection is the place of the God or Goddess of the earth and their holy council and the angels approaching grade 100.

All the heavens of the earth are very organized:

> *Think not, that my discipline is less systematic than that of a mortal general's army, or that the heavens of your God are permitted to run at loose ends, and without order or concert of action.*

> *Be reasonable, O Man, weigh these things according to your own observation and judgment, for there is not, in all the heavens, any wide departure from what you have in some form a counterpart-resemblance on earth.*

As above, so below.

Etherea

The highest level of spiritual existence is known as *etherea*. It is the only place within the levels of existence that does not dissipate. Mortal worlds come and go and so do atmospherean worlds, but the etherean worlds do not for they are truly the abode of the immortals. Etherea is the space beyond the vortex of a planet. It is all the "empty" space of the universe. This is the dwelling place of the angels who have graduated from a mortal world and are one hundred percent in service to the Creator. These angels are called *ethereans*, and they dwell throughout all space in our galaxy and beyond as immortal beings of light:

> *Jehovih said: "Think not that the vault of the firmament is nothing; for there I have created etherean worlds of sizes equal to the corporeal worlds, but they are independent of them.*

> *These are My kingdoms, prepared for the spirits of men and women and children, whom I bring forth into life on corpor. Nor are My etherean worlds alike in density or motion, but*

of different consistencies, that they may be suitable for the varied advancement of My children.

The earth is one of many nurseries throughout the universe for the cultivation of the gods and goddesses. The following quote from *the Oahspe* is a conversation between an etherean Orian Chief in charge of the earth and an etherean Chief surveying many galaxies beyond our own:

> *What time has your journey yet before you? Ctu said: Five hundred thousand years! Then Fragapatti inquired how many star-worlds (earths) Ctu had so far passed on his journey and Ctu said: Twenty thousand star-worlds we have passed, some smaller than this red star (our earth), and some ten thousand times larger.*

They go on to discuss that Ctu has seen them in all their stages of development from creation to dissolution. Then Ctu said:

> *The mortal desires to become a spirit, then his ambition is to become an etherean, next an Orian, next a Nirvanian, next an Oe'tan and then to travel in the surveys of magnitudes throughout the universes.*

We are immortals at the beginning of our journey into forever.

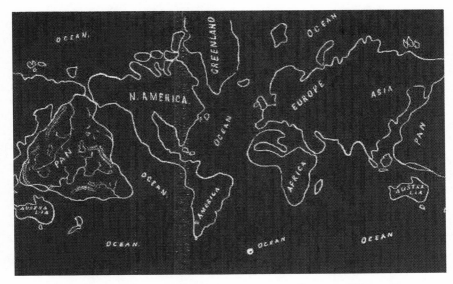

The Earth before the Flood, Twenty-Four Thousand Years Ago

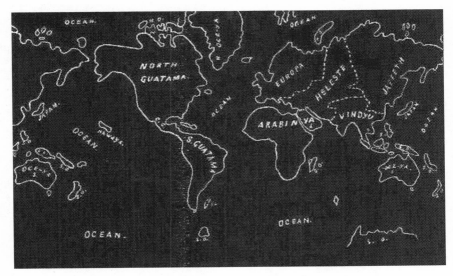

The earth after the sinking of Pan

NOTES:

The Book of Ben

Sometimes called the Book of the Nine Entities, Who are the Tree of All Light

God said: These are the nine entities, or, according to the ancients, Jehovih and His eight children, His Sons and Daughters. And these are the same, which in all ages, poets and philosophers have made to speak as the family of the universe. Through them, I speak. Jehovih is the Light, that is, Knowledge. The manifestation of Knowledge in Man is Jehovih. The growth of wisdom in Man, as the earth grows older, is the tree of light.

Book of Ben

The Book of Ben is a dialogue between Man and the nine entities. The main theme of this book relates to Man's striving for knowledge and understanding. Spirit constantly calls Man to look past the physical world, past books and beliefs, to find true knowledge. The Book of Ben unravels Man's concepts of what nature is, what the Creator is, what truth is, and what is real. The Book of Ben is written differently than the other books in Oahspe, as it is a dialogue between forces that influence our lives. If it seems confusing, stay with it and it will eventually make sense.

God speaks to us and teaches us about life through nine major avenues. These aspects, or beings, are called *the nine entities*.

Jehovih is the Creator, All That Is, Divine Presence, the Great Spirit:

> *Jehovih said: I am Knowledge; come to Me. I am the Unseen. Behold yourself, O Man! Can you put your finger on the place and say: Here is knowledge? Has wisdom bulk and a place?*

Tae is the highest overall expression of humanity. The other aspect of Tae is the universal voice. Tae presents itself as the Creator speaking through humanity in writings and other forms of inspiration. The voice of Tae only appears in the Book of Inspiration. It is listed in the Book of Ben because it is a part of the family of the universe:

These are the words of Tae, in Kosmon: I am Light; I am Central, but Boundless, said Jehovih.

Corpor is physical reality. It includes all matter and the realm of the five senses:

> *Jehovih has said: The corpor of Man I created as a womb for the es (spirit) of Man.*

Uz is the vanishing of things seen into the unseen. Hinduism calls this *Maya*. The physical world belongs to Uz. It is all that goes into dissolution, physical death. People who are caught up in the physical senses are called Uzians:

> *Uz said: O Man! Behold your folly! All things you see and hear and touch are my abode.*

Esfoma is the changing times; a sense of something coming; a feeling that things are going to change; an inner sense or knowing that a lot of external change means life is taking a turn and one's life is going to change:

> *Esfoma said: I am the signs of the times.*
> *By my face the prophets foretell what is to be.*
> *I am the living mathematics, the unseen progress of things speaking to the senses of Man.*
>
> *My name is: The Signs of The Times.*
> *Why have you, the inhabitants of the earth, and you angels of the heavens, not beheld me in my march?*

Es is spirit, the one that dwells within all the living in the physical world and the spirits or angels of the next world. It can also mean communications from the angelic worlds. It is also the spiritual dimensions after earth and their interactions with mortals:

> *Es said: Behold the utterances of the birds and the skipping of the lambs at play! These are the expressed love they have for the Creator.*

Ha'k is the entity of darkness. It is ignorance. It is a lack of light in the consciousness of people. Ha'k speaks only once in the Book of Ben to give a comparison between the vastness of the light and the smallness of the darkness:

> *Ha'k said: Who knows the boundary of Light? Behold, I cannot hide away from Him. What is my small corner compared with the All Light of etherea?*

Kosmon is the Age we are now living in, similar to the Age of Aquarius. Our solar system is moving through the Arc of Kosmon in our galaxy:

> *Kosmon said: Because Man lives on corporeal worlds, corpor is called son; but because Man in spirit lives in the es worlds, es is called daughter.*

> *Kosmon said: Why will you, O Man, search forever in matter for the cause of things? Behold, the unseen part of yourself rules over the seen.*

Seffas is the established. It is the laws that are established. It is Man's law:

> *Seffas said: My peace is forced peace. I am the light and the life. O vain Man! In the day you abuse the ancients; you send your son to college and enforce him to study the ancients.*

> *Your standing armies hold the nations of the earth in misery greater than did the temples and pyramids. And as for drunkenness and dissolute habits, and for selfishness, you are worse than the ancients.*

* * *

The Arc of Bon - Chapter I

Three thousand years ago the earth was traveling in the Arc of Bon. An Arc is a field of light. It reaches from one section of etherean lights to another. As our solar system travels through the galaxy it moves through different arcs approximately every three thousand years. Every arc has a different name because they are in different places in the galaxy and they have different qualities that affect the planets that pass through them. The earth is now traveling through the Arc of Kosmon and we are still in the beginning of the etherean lights of the kosmon era. The Arc of Bon had the energies required to bring the earth into its maturity over the last three thousand years. Before the Arc of Bon the people of the earth had fallen into darkness:

> *God said: Before the Arc of Bon the earth was rank.*
> *The seed of the tree of light had been planted many times, but the*
> *rankness destroyed it. In the time of the Arc of Bon, the earth reached*
> *maturity.*

In the past, the wisdom of Creator could only be received by a small number of people on earth because of the lack of consciousness of most people. The attempts to anchor the light or spiritual wisdom permanently on the earth had failed until the coming of the prophets Capilya, Moses, and Chine. Zarathustra had anchored spiritual knowledge nine thousand years ago that would not perish, but it stayed in a small corner of the world in the hands of a few people. Through the teachings of Capilya, Moses, and Chine the wisdom of the Light would spread across the world. The earth had reached a point of maturity and would not fall back into great darkness again.

(See *The Oahspe* for more information on the lives of Capilya, Moses, and Chine.)

The Prophets

In order for a person to be a prophet they must be pure enough in spirit and in body to receive the inspirations of the higher heavens clearly.

It usually takes six generations of mortals whose lineages have been managed by the angels for this to happen:

> *Jehovih said: I gave to the inhabitants of the earth Capilya, Moses, and Chine. Through them, the tree of light was made everlasting on the earth. The great peoples then knew I was God, and my word was with them.*

India, Egypt and China were the greatest countries on earth at that time, so God and the angels inspired marriages that would create a person within each of these countries that would be capable of hearing God's voice; Capilya for India, Moses for Egypt and Chine for China. We call them prophets or messengers of God. They were not God; they were the messengers of God and God is the messenger of the Creator.

Direct Experience

Jehovih makes it clear that if we want to experience the light of knowledge we have to go straight to the source like the true prophets of old:

> *Jehovih said: I am Knowledge; come to Me. I am the Unseen. Behold yourself, O Man! Can you put your finger on the place, and say: Here is knowledge? Has wisdom bulk and a place?*

Man is always questioning and seeking answers to life. How do things work and why? What happens after we die? How do we know we have a spirit? Es speaks and proclaims her presence within Man:

> *Es said: I am within your corpor; when your corpor molds into dust, behold, I am the es-Man, your real self. I am your spirit and, like a seed planted, I dwell within your corpor (body).*

The physical world of corpor is like kindergarten. Life on earth is our beginning. Corporeal life is for the growing of our spiritual selves. We are here to learn of the physical and the spiritual worlds.

Physical knowledge helps us understand the workings of life. Spiritual knowledge gives us wisdom and perception of the eternal in all things.

What we do and who we are becoming on earth prepares us for where we go when we die. We are growing our spirit every day with every thought and action.

If we ignore our spiritual development, if we do not care about our fellow beings on earth, or we cannot conceive of life after this earth life, then our spirit will be very weak and immature when we die. If our spirit is weak, we will be limited when entering the spiritual worlds. The more we understand the greater realities of existence, and we grow in awareness the stronger our spirit becomes. Then, when we pass over to the next world, it will be easier to move about and understand how to live in spirit, otherwise we will be starting as babies in a new world.

Life After Life

We are given three births. These are not reincarnations they are progressions of spiritual evolution away from the earth. Perhaps this is where the knowledge of spiritual development was distorted into reincarnations instead of stages of growing away from the earth. The first into physical form, the second into spirit when we pass through physical death and the third when our small self dies and we move into the etherean worlds:

> Jehovih has said: The corpor of Man I created as a womb for the es of Man. By death, behold, the es is born.

> Around about My corporeal worlds I placed atmospherea; for as the earth and other corporeal worlds provide a womb for the spirit of Man, so have I made atmospherea the substance for a womb for the souls of Man.

When we look up at night into the starry vault of heaven, we are in awe of the vastness of space and what might exist there:

> Jehovih said: Think not that the vault of the firmament is nothing; for there I have created etherean worlds of sizes equal to the corporeal worlds, but they are independent of them.

> These are My kingdoms, prepared for the spirits of men and women and children, whom I bring forth into life on corpor. Nor are My etherean worlds alike in density or motion, but of different consistencies, that they may be suitable for the varied advancement of My children.

Man asks why he is always searching and craving more understanding. The seeds of our immortality push us to look further and ask why:

> Jehovih said: Because I created your craving for light, you go forth searching. You are on a long road to the summit of All Light even Gods have not attained.

We receive from life according to our inclinations. If the material world is our focus, then the material world will be our teacher, and so it is with the spiritual world. Everything is divine:

> I have made two kinds of worlds: corporeal worlds and es worlds. A person who desires of corpor will receive from corpor, for he is My Son, in whom I am well pleased.

> A person who desires of es shall receive from es, for she is My Daughter, in whom I am well pleased.

The physical world is not evil it is the body of the Great Spirit. It is here for us to learn from. It is Creator in physical form. The spiritual world is not a place far away that we need not think about until we have to; it is the Creator's spirit. It lives inside of all physical reality.

The Unseen Source of All Things – Chapter II

The unseen rules the seen. The unseen holds the greatest power and is the most potent. The seen is impotent. The spirit rules over form. The spiritual worlds rule over the physical worlds. Spirit is the soul of all things and that which animates all things:

> *Jehovih said: I gave all power to the unseen to rule over the seen.*

Science looks at matter to explain the workings of life. Medicine looks at the physical function of the body to determine health. Some people look to material things to provide happiness:

> *Kosmon said: Why will you, O Man, search forever in matter for the cause of things? Behold, the unseen part of yourself rules over the seen.*

The Creator is the cause and effect, and the force behind everything. If we search for Creator inside the form of all things, then we may learn to truly understand them:

> *Jehovih said: I created all things, seen and unseen. My hand was forever stretched forth in work. I make and I dissipate everlastingly.*

The unseen creates the seen within ourselves and within all life. The Creator draws unseen energy into a vortex and drives the essence of matter into form. The spark of life awakens within the physical form by the presence of the Creator. Infinite and omnipresent beingness creates galaxies and planets, and gives us our first and last breath. It is the All Light that exists within everything:

> *Behold, I make a whirlwind in etherea, hundreds and hundreds of millions of miles across, and it drives to the center a corporeal world from that which was unseen.*

I blow my breath upon the planet, and lo, Man comes forth, inquiring:
Who am I and what is my destiny?

Man requests knowledge and truth beyond signs and symbols. God's reply is that all you see is not proof of your existence because you are made of light from the All Light:

> *Nor is there aught in your corporeal knowledge that you can prove otherwise, save it be your presence; and even that which you see is not your presence, but the symbol and image of it, for you yourself are but as a seed, a spark of the All Light that you cannot prove to exist.*

Man talks about knowing and loving the Creator. He wants to know how he can love that which he cannot comprehend. Es speaks of the beauty and goodness of this world as expressions of the presence of the divine that can lead us to understand the Creator:

> *Es said: Behold the utterances of the birds and the skipping of the lambs at play! These are the expressed love they have for the Creator.*

> *To rejoice because you are created; to seek after exalted rejoicing; to cultivate the light of your life; to turn away from dark things; these are to love your Creator.*

I AM Omnipresent - Chapter III

Mankind speaks with Uz wanting to understand how to live a good life:

> *Man said: Behold, I have struggled hard all my days, and met many crosses and losses. To provide for my son that he shall fare better, this is goodness.*

> *Uz said: Vain Man! You understand not the creations. Your trials, your losses and crosses, have built up your soul. To provide your son*

that he shall have no trials, nor losses nor crosses, will not be good for
him. This will not be goodness. Give him experience.

Mankind struggles to understand the laws of life and why they seem to contradict themselves:

Man said: Why, then, are there two laws: one to make the apple rise
up and grow on a tree, and one to make it fall down again. Is this
the creation? One law to pull one way, and another law in another
way? Can one law make one rose red, and another law make a rose
white? One law make one person good, and another law make another
person bad?

The nine entities challenge mankind's opinions and tell us that people do not understand the creation. We are lost in the symbols of things, as in pictures and books. We label pieces of our world and think we know what they are because we know their name. We think we know how things work because we can see them working. We look for the cause of things, but we do not see beyond the physical world. We have determined that life is mechanical, but we do not see what moves the mechanism. We agree upon laws that move creation. The laws of creation could be thought of as the hands of the great Mover, but we do not see or remember the one that moves all life:

Jehovih said: I make no laws. Behold, I labor with
My own hands. I am everywhere present.

Take a few moments to consider what the previous quote means. Allow your mind to let go of what you think is truth and consider what the Creator is saying. The Creator is all life, the quantum particle of energy within all matter and non-matter.

The dialogue continues as Man tries to comprehend how life works. By what law, by what cause and effect do things happen?

> *Man inquired: How can I know if a thing be of God or if it be of nature? What is Jehovih more than natural law?*
>
> *Corpor answered: What is nature, O Man? Why will you use a name for the members of my body? Behold, the trees are mine; the mountains and valleys; the waters and every living thing and everything that lives not; they are me. Why do you say nature?*
>
> *Now I say to you, the soul of all things is Jehovih; that which you call nature is but the corporeal part.*

Spirit and form, the unseen and the seen, dance the great dance of life, and the presence of the Divine is so complete that every breath, every thought, and every action is orchestrated by the presence of the Creator. How does a school of fish know to follow each other with split second turns and dives? We watch the movements that cannot possibly be thought out by a flock of birds dancing in the air. It is accomplished by the presence of the Creator, the I AM, the Ever-Present beingness that contains all that is within Itself. Perhaps one could say the flock of birds and school of fish are moving on the breath of the Elohim, on the breath of Allah, on the breath of the Tao, and the breath of the Great Spirit.

Eoih is the soul of all things, moving through everything in every moment. It is the great orchestral power of life:

> *God said: What have you gained by the word law, instead of the word Jehovih? If that that does a thing does it of its own accord, then it is alive, and wise withal. Therefore it is Jehovih. If it does it not of itself, then it is not the doer, but the instrument. How, then, can law do anything? Law is dead; and the dead do nothing.*

Men make laws, as betwixt themselves; these laws are rules governing action, but they are not action itself. Jehovih is action. His actions are manifested in things you see. He is Light and Life. All His things are a complete whole, which is His Person.

What is Truth? - Chapter IV

Man asks the Creator what he should believe if the things we think are true are not really truth:

If great learning has not proven anything real; if science is based on falsehood, and if there are no natural laws, should I not give up my judgment?

Is the soul of Man made of oxygen or hydrogen? Give me light that is real. I can say of what Man's mortal body is made.

Jehovih said: My divisions are not as Man's divisions. Behold, I create one thing within another. Neither space, nor place, nor time, nor eternity stands in My way. The soul is es. (Spirit)

What is it like to live in the spiritual worlds and how do the angels travel in the spiritual worlds?

And how does the soul of Man live in heaven? If the es-Man has feet and legs, how does he walk? Have his arms changed into wings? Or does he ride on the lightning?

God said: Already your soul goes forward, but it cannot take your body with it. Your corporeal judgment cannot cope with spiritual things.

Corporeal judgment cannot cope with things of the spirit. This is one of the main reasons why so many people have difficulty grasping spiritual reality. Only our spiritual being can conceive of spiritual things. If we have not developed our spirit then we will have difficulty understanding things of a spiritual nature.

Our thoughts and deeds on earth develop our capacities to function in the spiritual worlds. We are driven on earth by our desires, and in the heavens, as well:

As thought travels, so is it with the spirits of the dead. When you have quit your corporeal body, behold your spirit will be free; wherever you desire to go, you will go. Nevertheless you will go only as thought goes. And when you have arrived at the place, you will fashion, from the surroundings, your own form, hands and arms, and feet and legs, perfectly.

The Gods build not only themselves, but plateaus for the inhabitation of millions and millions of other souls raised from the earth.

Man asks why he was born in darkness without knowledge and the ability to perceive the Light:

Kosmon answered: Had you not craved for light, you had not been delighted to receive light. Had you been created with knowledge, you could not be an acquirer of knowledge. Had the Creator given you angels to be forever giving you light, then they would be slaves.

Liberty is the boon of men and angels; the desire for liberty causes the soul of Man to come out of darkness.

Whether on the earth or in the heavens, we must learn to discipline ourselves, to become strong and determined in overcoming that which holds us down. We can focus our thoughts in order to manifest what we desire. We can learn from the past and live in the present:

Whoever feels that he has no need for exertion grows not in spirit. He has no honor on the earth or in the heavens because of that. To make Man break away from all the past and live by the Light of the Ever Present, is this not the wisest labor?

How Do We Find Truth? - Chapter V

Man speaks of his delight in obtaining knowledge. The Creator speaks about how only knowledge that Mankind can comprehend is given to him:

> *God said: Was not this answered to you? According to the light that Man was capable of receiving, so was he answered.*
>
> *Man inquired: But why was not the truth told? Why the six days? And why the rib?*
>
> *God said: That which Man can accept, and is good for him, is given to him. That which Man cannot comprehend, cannot be revealed to him.*

Humanity has now reached a level of consciousness in which we can understand more of the workings of life in this world and the next.

Man struggles to understand which way to go and how to live:

> *Man said: How shall Man find light, knowledge, wisdom, truth? Is there no all teacher? Learning is void, because based on false grounds? The senses are void, because they themselves are perishable and imperfect? Where shall Man find a true standing point to judge from?*
>
> *Uz said: All you see and hear, O Man, are but transient and delusive. Even your own corporeal senses change every day. Today you try to raise up your son in a certain way; but when you are old, you will say: Alas, I taught him differently from what I would now.*

Throughout the Book of Ben, the main theme is that what we perceive as truth today is likely to change tomorrow. What we think is wisdom and knowledge also changes. What we think is natural law is not a law that applies always to everything. All of these are attempts to explain life. But life is changing and moving all the time.

Knowledge, truth, and natural law are the presence of the Divine in each moment, moving and creating and dissipating all things. Truth and wisdom can only be found in the present. All of life lives by the Light of the Ever Present: Eoih. By living in the moment and realizing the constant state of change and newness that life presents to us, we learn to judge for ourselves the truth of each day, each experience, and each thought:

> God said: Man, you shall judge yourself as to what you shall do. Within every Man's soul, Jehovih has provided a judge that will soon or late become triumphant in power.

Man abandons reasons and arguments and makes a covenant with the Creator regarding how to live in order to be in concert with the Creator and find the Light and the truth in each day. The way becomes very simple:

> Only will I labor and do good, and be in peace within my own soul and with my neighbors, and glorify You.

God Speaks about Creator -Chapter VI

God shows the way for each of us to commune with the All Light. We are all capable of a direct relationship with the Creator, according to our desire and our openness to the presence of the divine:

> He is the same today and forever. The prophets of old found Him, so also can you. But He comes not to the denier, nor to the disapprover. He who will find His Person must look for Him. He who will hear His Voice must hearken. Then comes light.

> All argument is void. There is more wisdom in the song of a bird than in the speech of a philosopher. The first speaks to the Almighty, proclaiming his glory. The second plods in darkness.

By my hand were the ancient libraries burnt,
to draw Man away from darkness.

Books and philosophy can point the way, but spiritual understanding comes through direct experience of the Creator. Direct experience can only happen in the present when we are open and reaching to hear "Eoih's Voice in the Wind:"

Kosmon said: What has great learning found that is valuable?

Shall learning, like riches, be acquired for one's own selfish gratification?

If a rich person with his horded wealth does little for the resurrection of Man, how much less does the learned person with a head full of knowledge?

If neither feeds nor cloths the sick and distressed, nor stays the debauchery and drunkenness of the great multitude.

God shows that living in the past or the future is not a good way to navigate through the present, because the Creator is the Ever Present:

What healed the sick yesterday will not tomorrow. Philosophy that was good yesterday is folly today. Religions that were good for the ancients are worthless today. Crime and pauperism grow up in the heart of them, even worse than in the regions of the earth where they are not preached. The physicians have not lessened the amount of sickness on the earth. The lawyers have not lessened the rascality of the wicked or depleted the number of defrauders.

If we can't rely on past knowledge, where do we find the answers to life's questions? Where do we look for guidance? Where is the compass that can show us the way through this life? The Ever Present is the compass. Each moment is eternal, and only in the present can we discern what is needed. Write your obligations on the calendar or a list of things to do, but keep your attention and your awareness in the present moment as you fulfill your earthly obligations.

Changing Times - Chapter VII

Esfoma speaks about change, about the ongoing march of the Ever Present. This perspective can be frightening. Where is the stability? Where is the security of knowing that the sun will rise in the morning and there will be air to breathe each day, food to eat, a place to live, and, most of all, safety in the midst of constant change? We can learn to read the signs of change as they occur, and this will help us see and understand what is unfolding in our lives:

> *Esfoma said: I am the signs of the times. By my face the prophets foretell what is to be. I am the living mathematics, the unseen progress of things speaking to the senses of Man. My name is: The Signs of The Times. Why have you, the inhabitants of the earth, and you angels of the heavens, not beheld me in my march?*

History gives us many examples of how the civilizations of Man come and go, and the gods that people once worshipped are forgotten:

> *I called out in the days of the pyramids: O you kings and mighty ones! Behold the signs of the times! And you people of great learning, give ear; a voice speaks in the wind!*

> *Behold, Osiris and Isis shall go down. Anubi shall not judge the people of the Almighty! Then I come forth over all the land. Man begins to doubt, then to disbelieve, and then to deny the popular Gods and Saviors of his forefathers.*

Throughout the thousands of years of the history of Man, humanity has worshiped the Creator by many names and worshipped many gods and false gods. *The Oahspe* talks of the Gods and the false gods of the earth. It talks of the reign of the false gods and how they always turn toward the destruction of humanity for the increase of their own power. When this happens, the true Gods intervene and the kingdoms of the false gods fall:

> *I sent a storm into colleges of learning; the wise professors held up their heads and said: I doubt the person of Osiris! I doubt Isis! Are they merely a principle?*

> *The prophets looked here and looked there. They said: Behold the signs of the times! Let us measure the increase in the growth of skepticism to these ancient Gods. They said: Osiris shall go down, and so shall Isis and Anubi, and Baal, and Ashtaroth, and Thammus. But the kings heard not; they called their councils for stern legislation.*

All the edifices that we build must perish at some point. When what we have built can no longer hold the truth of the present moment, it will cease to exist.

> *Jehovih has said: All things are like a tree, which springs up from a little seed to become mighty; which bears fruit for a season and then falls and is turned to dust.*

> *One by one, My Gods and My false Gods rise up and are powerful for a season, and then are swept away in Esfoma's hands. Behold My thousands of Saviors, which I have sent to raise up the inhabitants of the earth. Where are they this day?*

> *I give to mortals Gods and Lords and Saviors, according to the time and place of the earth in My etherean heavens, so bestow I them. But when they have fulfilled their time, lo, I take away their Gods and Lords and Saviors. Not suddenly, nor without signs of the times of their going.*

The Battle of the False Gods - Chapter VIII

The path of humanity's evolution is one of repeated upliftment and then decline, as the All Light evolves humanity into higher and higher levels of awareness and spiritual development. During the last two cycles of three thousand years, there have been high-raised angels in charge of the lower heavens. They started out with the best of intentions and then fell before the lure of power, becoming false gods. At the beginning of the Arc of Bon, about three thousand years ago, these fallen angels were called *the four heads of the Beast,* and their names were *Dyaus, Lord God, Osiris,* and *Te-in.* They divided up the major areas of population in the Middle East, India, and China and became the main gods of the earth.

Toward the end of this cycle of three thousand years and before the Arc of Kosmon in the mid1850s, the four heads of the Beast were *Ennochissa the false Brahma; Kabalactes the false Budha; Thoth the false Gabriel* and *Looeamong the false Kriste.* These false gods or fallen angels established Brahmanism, Buddhism, Mohammedanism, and Christianity. The true Brahma lived six thousand years ago and the true Budha was called Sakaya and he lived approximately two thousand five hundred years ago.

When higher angels fall to false gods, they set to work building religions to gather followers who will populate their kingdoms when they die. These spirits of the dead become willing servants of the false gods because they believe the false gods are the Creator or the highest god. The false gods enslave the newly dead with the lies of their greatness.

When the earth passes through the etherean lights, all beings, mortal and spirit, are awaken to the truth of the conditions around them. Whether it is a false god or a false government, the darkness is all the same. All beings desire truth and freedom and the coming of the Light heralds this change. The deceptions of the ruling powers cannot endure the Light. The false gods fall to anarchy and destruction, as do the false governments of Man.

During the Arc of Bon the kingdoms of the false gods became more and more difficult to manage because they were not uplifting the spirits in their charge. The false gods then started quarreling amongst themselves about who had the greatest kingdoms and the greatest power. The quarreling led to aggression, and they began to fight with each other. This sounds like the earth at this time with the world leaders quarreling amongst themselves. The stronger the light of the Arc of Bon became the greater the fighting between them:

> *Es said: The light of Jehovih touched on the earth and the heavens about were stirred to the foundation. Things past were moved forward. His voice was from the depth of darkness to the summit of All Light.*

When a world moves into the etherean lights, the darkness of its people and its heavens are stirred up as the light exposes the shadows. The call went out from Creator for all His children to awaken from the darkness, and His children, both mortal and angel, were awakened:

> *Jehovih said: Bring forth the legions of earth and heaven! Summon up the dead! Let the living rejoice! My kingdom is at hand. And the dead came forth, clothed in the raiment of heaven, and they walked upon the earth. Face to face, they talked with the living, proclaiming the fullness of Jehovih and his everlasting kingdoms.*

This call to awaken is given by Creator at the beginning of every passage into the etherean lights. It is a reunion for the living and the dead, and it brings up the shadows and the light for all to see. Those whose lives were cut short by war and those who suffered from the wars come forward in these times to vent their anger:

Then rose the cloud of darkness, higher and higher; the poisonous smell and damnable tricks of hada (lowest heavens) belched forth in terrible blackness.

The spirits of those slain in war, delirious, mad, and full of vengeance; and those whose earth-lives had bound them in torments; and those who lived on earth to glut themselves to the full in abhorrent lust, came assuming the names of Gods and Saviors.

As the light continued to increase, the darkness fell further into madness and the heavens and the earth were at war. As above, so below is the axiom by which we can often judge the source of things. The wars in heaven create the wars on earth. The hells in heaven perpetuate the wars on earth.

The false gods inspired their followers on earth to destroy each other, and the false gods fought with each other. The wars on earth raged across the lands as the wars in heaven continued:

Still struggled the beast, awful in the smoke and dust of his bloodstained mantle, till the earth around became as a solemn night before a battle of death. Rattling bones and empty skulls, with gnashing teeth, all stained with human gore, made hideous by the portentous omen, caused angels and men to stand appalled.

Moses, Capilya, and Chine lived during the cycle of the Arc of Bon. These prophets led their people out of the reign of darkness and into the light of freedom:

Jehovih answered to His faithful sons and daughters, the living and the dead: Bring forth the legions of earth and heaven! Summon up the dead! Let the living rejoice! My kingdom is at hand! My chosen shall be free! The beast, rattling his hideous bones with bated breath, watched to see the great awakening light of the tree of Jehovih!

Osiris was the last of remaining false gods after the wars in heaven. His last effort to maintain his kingdom was when he influenced the Pharaoh to destroy all the Faithists in Egypt. His efforts failed, as the Creator guided Moses and his people out of Egypt.

Bringing Peace to the Earth - Chapter IX

The earth was now past the etherean lights of the Arc of Bon and new angels replaced the false Dyaus, Lord God, Osiris, and Te-in. The new angels set to work to uplift humanity from the destruction of these previous false gods. The people of the earth were inspired to return to peace and to the Creator. During this process, many of the old ways were put aside:

> *Jehovih said: When the Gods have fulfilled their time in earth and heaven, behold I put them away. In the overthrow of the departing Gods, behold, there is the beginning of a new springtime in Jehovih's seasons.*

> *He plants a new tree in His garden; it is a tree of new light for the righteous. His chosen go out, away from the fleshpots of the past, and they have neither kings nor emperors, only the Almighty!*

One mark of the Faithists—people who are attuned to the Creator—is that they do not have or rely on kings or rulers; they govern themselves. When the forefathers of America broke away from the rule of England, they were inspired by the angels to create a land that was ruled by the people, for the people. Yes, this country has changed in many ways, but the Light of America will hopefully prevail.

The Oahspe has a wonderful section on America and how the angels assisted the forefathers to create the United States of America and to eliminate slavery. See the Book of Es in *the Oahspe*.

Wisdom for Our Times - Chapter X

God calls to Man to become aligned to the Creator and seek to live in the present, not hanging onto the past. Life is not static or ridged, it flows, constantly changing and moving to create anew in each moment:

> God said: Here is wisdom, O Man: To be observant of all things and adapt yourself to that on Jehovih's side.
>
> To obtain great learning that applies to the resurrection of your soul in comprehending the works of the Almighty.
>
> To suffer not yourself to be conceited in the wisdom of the moderns over the ancients, nor of the ancients over the moderns.
>
> The Creator created Man wisely for the time of the world in which Man was created. You are for this era, and not for the past.
>
> The ancients were for the past era, and not for the present. To know the present, to be up with the signs of the times, is to see Jehovih's hand.

God warns us that when mankind makes a god of wealth or science or great learning then civilization is about to make a big change. When mankind becomes focused on the corporal world more than the spiritual world, even to the point of denying the presence and influence of the spiritual worlds, then the Creator will cause change on the earth:

> Make not a God of riches, or of your supposed
> sciences and learning.
> For in the time you see men doing these things, behold,
> that is the time of a cyclic coil in the great serpent.

When mankind moves away from being in right relationship to the Creator, the Orian Chiefs and Chieftess of etherean will make the necessary changes in the course of our solar system to bring us back into harmony with the Great Spirit. The cyclic coil in the great serpent refers to the course of our solar system through the galaxy. The serpentine path of our solar system presses in on itself and makes a coil within the vortex of the solar system. As the great serpent is condensed great changes come to the world.

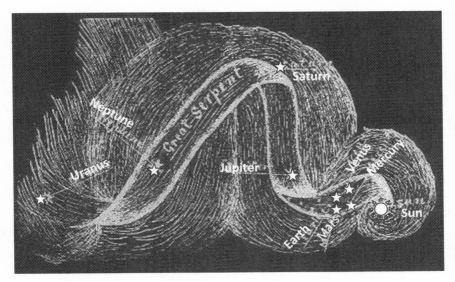

The Great Serpent

Our solar system is called the Great Serpent because of its serpentine path through the galaxy.

"The length of the great serpent is approximately 1500 million miles long." (The Oahspe Bible, Book of Fragapatti, page 219, chapter XVII, verse 4.)

"The numbers of the beast shall be sixty-six, and six hundred and sixty-six, and the parts thereof. Because in the coil of the cycle, behold the distances are two-thirds of a circle, whether it be a hundred or a thousand, or three times a thousand. Jehovih rolleth up the heavens and braideth the serpents of the firmament into His cyclic coil. He is the circle without beginning or end."

The Book of Ben ends with an explanation of how to attune to the Creator and navigate through times of change:

To learn how to live, to rejoice, and to do good, and make your neighbor rejoice also: this is wisdom. Let these be your loves and the glory of your speech, and you shall learn to prophesy concerning the ways of Jehovih.

NOTES:

The Book of Judgment

Being the Grades and Rates of Mortals and Angels in the Light of God, as the Word Came to Es, Daughter of Creator

For I will make Man understand that he will accept nothing from angels or mortals because of the name professed. On the merit only of wisdom and truth, and such good doctrines as raise people up out of darkness and poverty and crime, will they accept either spoken or written words.

God said: There will be a day of judgment to you, O Man. Sooner or later, you will take the matter into your own hands, and you will look into your own soul to judge yourself. This is to all people; none can escape it.

God Speaks - Chapter I

God speaks about himself and the assignment he was given by Jehovih:

Hear the words of your God, O Man! I am your
elder brother of tens of thousands of years' experience. Profit
from my wisdom, and learn the discourse of your God.

Imagine listening to a being who is tens of thousands of years old, and the level of awareness the being must have. The Creator commands God to teach humanity about Him and about the heavens:

And you will reveal to mortals the plan of My worlds and as to who
you are and the method of your inspiration and dominion on the earth
and her heavenly kingdoms.

In the beginning of the present era of kosmon, the gates of heaven are to be opened so that Man can learn about the spiritual dimensions. What are the gates of heaven? They may be the Pearly Gates. Perhaps these gates, or veils, represent divisions between the spiritual worlds or dimensions. As was mentioned earlier, a spirit or angel can only live within the energy field or dimension that they are suited for. These gates may be like borders that divide areas of higher and lower dimensions. They may be the borders of the changing degrees of light between dimensions. In the world of music, the flats and sharps divide the whole notes from each other. We could use this analogy to describe the existence of dimensions as whole notes and the veils or gates of heaven as the sharps and flats that separate them.

The Workings of the Angels of Heaven

More and more people are seeing and experiencing the presence of spirit beings. There are even ghost buster organizations that look for spirits to prove their existence:

You will keep open the gates of heaven for a season, and the spirits of the dead will commune with mortals, good and evil, wise and foolish. And mortals will see them and talk with them, face to face; and they will recognize their own kin, sons and daughters, fathers and mothers, brothers and sisters, the dead and the living.

During this period of increased light, the angels can manifest all kinds of miracles. The miracles are to help show Man how the spiritual realms interact with the earth. Some of the interactions are for good and some are not:

And Man will understand that even as plants and trees and fish and serpents can be wielded by My angels, so also can virus and pestilence be carried by angels of darkness to cast mortals in death.

Mankind is to learn that how we live on earth sets the course for our lives in the spiritual realms. How we live also attracts spirits of like mind. If we are focused on accumulating wealth, we will attract spirits who are bound by greed. If we are involved in recreational drugs, we will attract spirits who enjoy the same activity:

And you will suffer evil spirits and all manner of drujas, and vampires and engrafters, to come, and manifest to mortals, that they may know, whereof My revelations unfold the matters of earth and heaven.

For Man will understand what I mean by the words: As you live on the earth, so will you reap in heaven.

False Gods and earthbound souls are notorious for using miracles to give validity to their existence. The ability to perform a miracle is not considered a great ability. Miracles are often used by earthbound souls to get the attention of mortals. Humanity has reached a level of discernment in which a miracle is not necessary for us to discern whether a person or information has merit:

For I will destroy the worship of all Gods and Lords and Saviors on the ground of miracles.

We often go through life as if we are in a perpetual circus, reaching out for the newest entertainment, looking to the latest famous person, wanting to have a bigger and better toy to entertain us, and on it goes. The spiritual arena can be the same kind of circus. People go from one medium to another seeking confirmation that the spiritual worlds are real and looking for good news. Is it wrong to seek understanding? This is not a bad desire, but we must learn discernment when seeking information from the spiritual realms, just as we have to be discerning with a lawyer, a doctor, or a politician:

And you will suffer to fall in darkness such mortals as consult the angels in regard to riches, or to marriage, or to self, or for curiosity, or frivolity, or for anything of an earthly nature for profit's sake. They will prosper for a season, but end in being confronted with folly and falsehood.

And whoever asks for the spirits of great people, send him to be deceived by drujas and all manner of lying spirits. And who ever asks of the sar'gis (mediums) for great people, or for Moses, or Jesus, or Kriste, or for any well-known name, as applied to ancient times, suffer him to be answered by evil spirits and deceivers.

This last quote gives us some basic rules of discernment for the spiritual realms. If we seek wisdom by calling on a one-time mortal, we might receive all kinds of information from ignorant and deceiving spirits.

How are we to seek wisdom from the spiritual realms and not end up with lower, deceiving spirits? In the spiritual worlds, like attracts like. According to the lifestyle a person lives, and their intentions they will attract similar spiritual beings. The location a person is in when they seek spiritual wisdom can also influence what kind of angels will respond. Be clear about what you are seeking and seek knowledge from the source of all knowledge, the Creator. Be free of alcohol, drugs, and tobacco. Live in a peaceful place. Spend time with others who are seeking more than something fun to do. If you want to connect with deceased loved ones, then do, but don't make a habit of it, or you will place them in bondage.

What is our intention when we reach out for things or people, knowledge or power? Is it to serve the greater good of our fellow Man and life on earth? Is it to serve more than only ourselves? This is the key when seeking wisdom. 'Divine Presence, open my heart and mind to thy presence in this moment and in everyone.'

There comes a time in the evolution of all sentient life on worlds such as earth when self-serving no longer works. It will be in such glaring opposition to the evolution of the consciousness of all life that people will no longer be able to live in a self-centered existence. It appears that the earth is undergoing such a transition and evolving toward higher consciousness at an accelerated pace. We are graduating from juvenile consciousness to adulthood. This graduation is a requirement, not an option, because humanity has a great destiny. We must move forward towards fulfilling that destiny:

> In all former cycles, My Gods had to deal with separate divisions of the earth; My revelations were to each, for a special time, which is now at hand. I have prepared this land (North America) untrammeled with Gods and Saviors and Lords, enforced by the sword, so that My revelations of this day will be published and not suppressed.

Humanity is coming into a new level of consciousness in which we can understand new concepts about the universe and the presence of the spiritual worlds. We are about to graduate from thousands of years of fear and ignorance into a time of lasting peace and enlightenment.

Can we let go of the small, selfish part of ourselves, our fears and misconceptions, and take responsibility for our thoughts and actions? This evolutionary shift will require a dismantling of many of the things that have held our present concepts of reality together. With this dismantling, there will be a greater awareness of the worlds around us, and our interaction with these worlds.

Who's Who in the Heavens?

How do we know what kind of spirits come to us? How do we know the true identity of a spirit or angel and where it comes from?

> And you will take great liars, and give them lying spirits to speak through them by inspiration and entrancement. And these spirits will profess the names of great persons long since dead. And they will manifest great oratory and wisdom and truth; but, nevertheless, their preaching will be of little avail for righteousness sake, or for good works.
>
> For the spirits, who speak through them will be of the first resurrection, and know not Me nor the higher kingdoms. Verily they will be of the same order as the spirits who minister in the churches and temples, being such spirits as have not yet been delivered up from the earth.

We must learn to discern who to listen to by the message given and its ability to help others. It is not about names and popularity, it is about wisdom. We must learn to judge clearly.

The angels of the first resurrection are very interactive with the earth and often act individually with mortals. Their wisdom is limited by their personal beliefs and their motives:

> And some will say: Hear me, for I am God! Some will say: Hear me, for I am the Lord! Some will say, Hear me, for I am Creator! And

others will profess the names of mortals who had great power on the earth. Send them to do these things.

Many people receive information from spirit beings who call themselves by a name. It gives them a sense of personal connection to the spirit. It is also a clear sign that the spirit is of the inorganic heavens upon the earth. Spirits closest to the earth are bound to the earth and limited in their understanding of the heavens. Usually they do not know there are higher worlds. They can be reassuring and helpful. So can a mortal. However, the merit of the message should be the basis of our acceptance of the information from anyone, mortal or immortal:

For I will make Man understand that he will accept nothing from angels or people because of the name professed.

A continuous theme in *Eoih's Voice in the Wind* is letting go of our worship and acceptance of what someone says because of who they are or where the information has come from:

On the merit only of wisdom and truth, and such good doctrines as raise people up out of darkness and poverty and crime, will they accept either spoken or written words.

We can learn about the spiritual worlds through direct communication with the spiritual worlds. We all have the ability to communicate with the next world and the spirits that live there. These communications can confirm for us the existence of life after death. No book or mortal can confirm for another the existence of life after death. Only direct experience with spirits of the other worlds can confirm this reality.

Many people are afraid of séances and Ouiji boards, and rightly so, because they can attract lower spirits who want to cause mischief. However, they can be a way to experience the presence of discarnate beings. Coming together in small groups for spiritual communion is another way to connect with the spiritual worlds.

We experience the presence of spirits in our everyday lives but are usually not aware of it. We will hear a comment or a suggestion telepathically that seems to come 'out of the blue'. It might be a spirit companion or a passing spirit. It could be one's own mind or the thoughts of another mortal nearby. As we develop an awareness of the spiritual worlds, we must also develop a deeper awareness of ourselves in order to discern where such information comes from.

Service

Many good people are trying to come together to help others, but their endeavors fail. We all need to learn humility and true service if we want to manifest good works:

> *And they will try to organize to carry out good works, but they will fail. For many will desire to be leaders, being under the influence of selfish considerations, desiring the applause of people. And they will profess freedom, but they will not pledge themselves to any sacrifice, either of money or opinion for sake of the public good.*

God gives us a list of the ways in which we can succeed in serving humanity and the earth at this time:

> *But in the time of the light of My revelations, you will raise up a few, here and there, capable of the All Light. And these, you will cause to form a basis for My kingdom on earth,*
>
> *And they will forswear all Gods and Lords and Saviors, but profess Me, the Great Spirit, Creator.*
>
> *And they will pledge themselves to one another in fullness, as brothers and sisters, holding their possessions in common.*

They will live for the sake of perfecting themselves and others in spirit, and for good works.

They will not eat fish nor flesh of any creature that breathed the breath of life.

And keep the seventh day as a day of communion with Me and My angel hosts, with rites and ceremonies explanatory of all the doctrines in the world.

They will practice good for evil; non-resistance to persecution and abuse and abjure war; even, if necessary, by submitting to death rather than take part in war.

And they will become an organic body in communities of tens and twenties and hundreds and thousands.

But they will have no leaders, only their Creator; but be organic, for sake of good works.

They will not go about preaching for sinners to go to repentance, nor preaching for charity to the poor.

They will go themselves about gathering up sinners, and the poor and helpless and orphans and bring them into comfortable homes, teaching them how to live to be a glory to Me and My kingdoms.

To such persons will My angels from the second resurrection come, and minister in My name for the joy of the earth.

The above quote is a tall order, but it would certainly solve a lot of our present problems on earth. It is possible to live another way, but we are the ones who must make it happen.

What does the above quote mean when it says for us to be organic? This is not talking about the quality of the food we eat. This quote is talking about aligning one's life to be in harmony with the organic heavens that are organized and communal. The heavens that lay upon the earth are inorganic and everyone is for themselves.

Like attracts like in the spiritual worlds. When we learn to live as the higher angels live, then they can help us grow and make the earth a wonderful place for everyone:

> *Neither will any other people in all the world escape the place of the first resurrection.*

> *Be they kings, or queens, or beggars, or Brahmins, or Buddhists, or Kriste'yans, or Mohammedans, or any other pretenders in heaven or earth.*

> *Behold, the day of preaching and professions are at an end. I will have practice only.*

Spiritual Communion - Chapter II

If a person would like to connect with the higher heavens and the spiritual beings who live there, we need to come together in groups with the intention of relating to the higher heavens. In this way, we can gain the ability to directly experience the higher worlds:

> *God, ambassador of Creator, said: You will assemble for the communion of angels, regularly, and maintain communication with them. For in no other way can you demonstrate the immortality of the soul. Do this in the name of Creator, and for spiritual light in regard to spiritual things.*

> *Remembering that the humblest prayer, even with weak words, if given with a full heart, is as strong to Creator as the best oratory.*

When people come together for communion with the higher beings of the second resurrection, they can have various experiences. Some may just be uplifted and some could be inspired to speak, others may experience entrancement and some a state of being in which a person allows a spirit to speak through them. This does not mean being taken over by an evil spirit against your will. These abilities are natural human capacities:

> But this will happen to many: Learning to speak by entrancement or by inspiration, they will imagine themselves controlled by certain angels, when, in fact, it is only their own spirit, eliminated from the corporeal senses.

> Others, being influenced, will imagine it is themselves and not an angel, whereas it is an angel speaking through them. This was the case of Ka'yu (Confucius). Both are good, and will be practiced.

> Let no Man concern himself as to whether it is the spirit of himself or an angel, for it is only the subject uttered which is of value. In this day, all things will stand on their own merit, and not on a supposed authority.

Removing the spirit-self from the corporeal (physical) self refers to the ability of a person's spirit to leave the physical body while the physical body remains alive and well. This is referred to as an *out-of-body experience*. The physical body is usually in a reclining or sitting position, and may appear to be asleep. Sometimes, the person is quiet, and sometimes they speak about what they are experiencing. The spirit of the person goes out of their physical body and may stay close at hand or travel to another place.

Environment plays a big part in everyone's life, and the activity of spiritual communion is no exception, so seek a clear and quiet place with others of like mind when practicing:

> It is wiser for the spiritual-minded to keep to themselves, especially when communing with Creator and His angels. For a greater wonder than these will follow:

*Some will enter the trance of the first resurrection, and go in spirit out of
the body, but only subjectively; others will enter the trance of the second
resurrection, and go in spirit out of the body objectively.*

What does it mean to go out of the body subjectively? This means that
a person maintains their earthly perspective, but sees the spiritual
worlds as if they are standing on the earth and looking into the
spiritual worlds. To go out in spirit objectively is to see or understand
the experience as if the person is in the spiritual world looking back
at earth.

The Uzians and the Faithists

There are three kinds of people on the earth: worldly people, the
believers, and the Faithists. Worldly people are completely involved
in the world and give little thought to life after death. The believers
understand that there is life after death, and they believe in the
spiritual worlds. They often strive to communicate with angels and
talk with spirits and psychics and all kinds of things, but they still live
worldly lives in which they are self-centered and perhaps even greedy
and indulgent. Both of these people are called Uzians. Faithists have
faith in the Creator. They believe there is life after death, and they
strive to live a good life, pursue spiritual development, and help others.
Faithists want to help the world become a better place for everyone.
The Faithists are considered the builders of the earth. The Uzians are
considered destroyers of the world:

*These three peoples, the world's people, the believers, and the Faithists,
have been in all ages of the world. Only the latter of them all practice
harmony and good works. Both of the others are resistants, quarrelers
and warriors, and disintegrators and breakers-down of all things.*

A Faithist is not prejudice with regard to race, color, dogma, or country. It is a term signifying a state of conscious evolution given to those who put the Creator first above all else. A person in this state of consciousness is no longer bound by fear, greed, and selfishness. They may experience these states, but they are able to rise above the pull of the lower self and reach out to help others grow:

> *Yet, the Faithists, having faith in the All Person, will ultimately possess the whole earth and make it a paradise of peace and love.*

How can a group of people possess the whole world? The world will evolve to a point where only Faithists can live on the earth. All people will have to evolve beyond the lower self to be able to withstand the increase of Light that is happening on the earth. Life on earth will then be considered to be "heaven on earth."

The Influence of Angels

The idea that there are angels interacting with us in our lives can be frightening and uncomfortable, or exciting and wondrous. For some people, it is hard enough to deal with the things they can see and touch, let alone acknowledge the presence of angels who can't usually be seen or touched. The important thing to remember is that the unseen rules the seen and the spiritual worlds interact with the physical world all the time.

The presence of angels affects us by association. When an angel is near they can think a thought and we receive it. When a guardian angel projects a thought toward us, or whispers in our ear, *we receive the communication to the degree to which we are clear enough to hear it.* The same is true when our own soul speaks to us.

How do we become clear enough to hear spirit? All people are born with spiritual faculties. For some, these abilities are open and active, and for some they are not. Many children have these gifts, but the people around them usually convince the child they are imagining things. This can be enough to close the faculty. As an adult, we can learn to open our spiritual abilities with diet, clean living, higher thoughts, and learning to listen for the subtle. In a sense, spiritual faculties are like muscles and lack of use will result in atrophy. Striving to strengthen a faculty often awakens it. Someone born into a family that has not been aware of other worlds for many generations often has a more difficult time opening their faculties. People born into lineages of seers and mystics often have their faculties already open.

How do spirits or angels influence us? They influence us by telepathic imprints. When we are shopping and all of a sudden we buy something we never intended to buy, we call it an "impulse." Perhaps it was, or perhaps a spirit close by wanted us to buy it because *they* liked it. When we have unpleasant (or pleasant) dreams, they can be our subconscious processing the experiences of our waking life or they could be the presence of spirits. Lower spirits are usually the cause of nightmares. Lower spirits often have sexual interactions with people in dreamtime. Lower spirits can also appear familiar in dreamtime or take on the guise of someone close to us, but the outcome of the dream will not be positive.

Ancestors often stay around family members until the family members no longer need them. They might stay for a short time to make sure their loved ones are okay. Sometimes ancestors think they know what's best for a loved one, and they will attempt to protect and influence them. This usually goes against a person's free will, but we mortals go against one another's free will all the time with our judgments. We impose our ideas and desires on each other, as do the spirits of the dead.

As we become clearer and more spiritually focused, we will know the difference between an impulse and an outside influence. Many people can hear or feel earthbound souls when the souls are hanging around. A spirit does not always impart wisdom or a good idea, nor do they always have our best interests at heart. Perhaps they do, and perhaps they don't. It is the responsibility of every person to become aware of the influences acting on them.

We know advertising does not always have our best interests at heart. Advertisements constantly influence us to do things we would not normally do. The spiritual dimension is no different. The good, the bad, and the in-between live in this world and in the next:

> *Let no Man say that only seers and prophets and such persons as work signs and miracles are under the influence of spirits; for even as much as these, so are other mortals under the dominion of spirits.*
>
> *Yea, the infidel, the disbeliever, the philosopher, the lawyer, the judge, the preacher, the fanatic, and all others, are more controlled by the spirits of the dead than by their own personal spirit.*
>
> *The more a Man's spirit is wrapped up in his own corporeality, the more is he subject to vampires and spirits of darkness.*

This is a little scary. Vampires and spirits of darkness may not look and act the way we've seen them in the movies, but they do exist. Vampires are earthbound spirits that live off the life force of a human being. Spirits of darkness delight in causing pain and suffering to mortals. They like to see people fight, so they try to induce fighting. Most of us have had the experience of being around someone who just makes us angry and we end up arguing with them. These types of people are often encumbered by spirits of darkness that enjoy causing people to fight with each other. They like to see people suffer, so they influence people to have accidents or become ill or harm another person, or kill an animal or a person. They love war and they love to incite people to war and destruction.

The reverse goes for good spirits. They want to help without imposing. They might drop an idea in our heads that really helps us on our journey. They might nudge us into situations that are wonderful.

Spiritual Progression

There is a spiritual progression within the evolution of consciousness. First, to understand that there is life after death, then to experience the presence of a spirit and know there is life after death, then to experience the higher realms, and, finally, to experience the presence of the Creator directly:

> Whoever has witnessed and knows of a truth that he has seen the spirits of the dead, that knowledge is impregnable. And who ever has entered the second resurrection, even though in mortality, that knowledge is impregnable.
>
> But, whoever has found the All Person, his knowledge is greater than all. And none below him can judge him. Neither can any Man attain to this knowledge, till he has passed through the other two conditions. No Man knows the Creator unless he has proven the communion of spirits.

No one can truly know the Creator unless we have experienced the presence of angels and know of our own experience that there are spiritual worlds around us. Many of us have a deep sense of the Creator and yet we have not had a direct experience with a spirit of the other worlds. This quote says that we cannot truly know the Creator if we have not experienced the Creators presence through interacting with the spiritual worlds. There is an important part of the Creator that we are missing if we do not consciously interact with the unseen worlds.

We would only know half of the Creator if we cannot experience the other worlds.

In the first resurrection, we bring with us all our perspectives and prejudices and our dreams and fears. Whatever our religious affiliation was on earth, it will be the same when we move into the spiritual worlds. There are many different churches and religions in the first resurrection; in fact all the religions are represented in the first resurrection. The first resurrection is filled with division and discord, as well as joy, love, and kindness. Remember that we all have the free will to evolve at our own rate. The Creator does not force us to believe one thing or another. It is we who chose our paths of evolution and the development of our consciousness. We can take as long as we like to let go of thoughts and actions that limit our evolution. Some spirits take hundreds of years to let go of hate and grudges and destructive behavior. It is their choice.

The second resurrection has different requirements than the first resurrection. God tells us that there will not be a house divided in the higher heavens:

> *Neither can any Man rise to the second resurrection till he has arisen to faith in the All One, Creator.*

> *Neither will the Brahmin, nor Mohammedan, nor Buddhist, nor Kriste'yans join in the second resurrection on earth or in heaven. For they have not the doctrine of unity; they are as a house divided against itself. Their colonies and communities will fail in all cases.*

> *There will be but one doctrine, which is Creator, the All Person, who is Ever Present; with good works done to others, with all of one's wisdom and strength.*

The world has been evolving through the first resurrection for a long time. The Age of Kosmon is about the world moving out of first resurrection consciousness and into second resurrection consciousness, while in mortal form. And when we do, the angels of the higher heaven will help us bring a lasting peace and prosperity to the world:

> *To such persons will My angels from the second resurrection come, and minister in My name for the joy of the earth.*

If we do not accomplish living beyond a self-centered life on earth, we will continue to work toward such a state when we enter the spiritual realms of the inorganic heavens nearest the earth. We will stay there until we have grown into service and are able to join with others in the first resurrection.

When we leave this world we can only live in the place we have earned during our lives on earth.

> *Whoever is not in My organic kingdoms on earth, will go into My inorganic kingdoms in heaven.*

God speaks about the Faithists as the chosen people. Being chosen is not about one race against another or one tradition being better than another. It is about people who have chosen to align themselves to the forces of goodness and serve the Creator. They have chosen to live in a way that is in harmony with life itself, and therefore life itself chooses them. It is in the choosing that we are chosen:

> *These latter are the chosen people of the Father of the Kosmon Era, and they will become supreme in all the world.*

The Faithest will become the majority of the people in the world. How appropriate to have those who care about the earth and all life to be the ones who are the caretakers of our world.

God Shows How to Worship Creator - Chapter III

We are beginning a new era on earth, and God/ Goddess of this world calls out to clear the slate, cut all ties to the past, and step into a new way of living, thinking, and relating:

> *Do you not think, O Man, that I am sufficient to the times and seasons. Or do you say that God spoke in the dark days of the earth, but now holds his tongue.*
>
> *Behold, I am your elder brother, even as a captain of the earth and her heavens for a season. As I am, even so were my predecessors in the time of the ancients: Ambassadors of the Most High, Creator whose power and wisdom are given to me, even after the same manner as are your earthly kingdoms governed and disciplined so that order may contribute to the resurrection of all of His created beings.*
>
> *First, I charge you that whoever says: God, God! calls in vain. I have not come to establish, but to abolish all Gods and Lords and Saviors among mortals. For what is past, is past.*

The old ways of relating to the Creator through prayer and confession and separate religions is over:

> *Nor have I provided resurrection in this world nor in my heavens above, except through good works done to others; and this is serving Creator, the All Person; and not because of any worship or confessions done before any of the idols on earth or in heaven.*

We've been evolving for thousands and thousands of years to reach this time in which we can let it all go and fall into the arms of the God. We can let go of our need for self-importance, material security, and power, in exchange for living lives of peace and service. We can let go of our fear in exchange for a relationship with life that allows us to live in our fullness, in happiness and in joy. We can live in gratitude for every day, every breath, and every opportunity to nourish the life around and within us:

> *But I give to all people one principle only, which is to serve Creator. This is broad enough for the redemption and resurrection of all people. And I will have none other.*

> *Seek, O Man, to believe in the All Person, who is Ever Present, whose eye is upon you, whose ear hears you; for He is the All One, who is the password to the highest of heavens.*

The best thing we can do is to care for each other:

> *Nor is there any redemption in heaven to the Brahmins, nor to the Buddhists, nor to the Kriste'yans, because of their prayers and confessions.*

But where good works have resulted in affiliation; and in lifting the people up out of misery and crime, the same is adjudged as worship of the Great Spirit, Creator

God Judges the Major Religions

We are accountable for what we have accomplished and what we have not accomplished. By their fruits you will know them:

> *Where the Brahmins, the Buddhists, the Ka'yuans, the Kriste'yans, or the Mohammedans have suffered a people to fall from knowledge into ignorance, or from virtue into vice, my judgment is against them.*

> *Where beggary and vagrancy and all manner of darkness have increased in any of the cities or countries of any of these idolaters, my judgment is against them.*

They will not excuse themselves nor escape my judgment by saying: O the true Brahmin, or the true Buddhist, or the true Mohammedan has not fallen. These that fell were such as did not embrace our doctrine in fullness of heart.

We have had thousands of years of religious doctrines and the world is still at war and we still live in fear and selfishness:

Wherefore, I have come to put these doctrines away and give them that which will prove itself potent in all the world. That, which I proclaim, will be proclaimed by the angels of the second resurrection, to all nations and peoples.

My light is not to one people only, save to the righteous, who serve the Creator by doing good to all people. In my sight, the nations of the divisions of the earth are as one people only, brothers and sisters.

The concept of separate religions and saviors is the consciousness of the first resurrection and this way of thinking is coming to an end:

And you may call on your idol at the gates of my heavens, but the gates will not be opened to you.

*For I will have no quarrel in my exalted kingdoms
in heaven as to Gods and Lords and Saviors.*

*Till you are washed clean of them; coming in spotless
white, a servant of the Most High, you cannot
withstand the light of my kingdoms in heaven.*

Until we raise our consciousness we will not be able to endure the higher lights of the higher heavens.

If we have been bound in the consciousness of separation while on earth, we will become earthbound spirits. When we evolve past separation and into the All Light through service to the Creator, we will be free to move on:

> *But you will return in spirit to the earth and abide in the church and temple of your chosen God, wandering about in stubbornness of heart, a prey to drujas and vampires and other angels of darkness.*
>
> *Have faith, O Man, in Him who created you alive; about Him there can be no mistake.*
>
> *Glorify Him by righteous works, having faith that even as He brought you into life, so will He provide for you, according to your just deserts.*

Earthbound Souls - Chapter IV

> *Hear the words of your God, O Man; I am your elder brother, the captain of heaven and earth.*

God tells us about how many earthbound souls there are in the inorganic heavens that are wandering the earth. Most of them are followers of the major religions. Remember, this text was written in 1882, and the numbers have undoubtedly increased:

> *Of Brahmin angels in the lowest of heavens, as wanderers on the earth, there are this day more than four billion.*
>
> *Of Buddhist angels in the lowest of heavens, as wanderers on the earth, there are this day more than seven billion.*
>
> *Of Ka'yuan angels in the lowest heavens, as wanderers on the earth, there are this day more than a billion.*
>
> *Of Kriste'yan angels in the lowest heavens, as wanderers on the earth, there are this day more than three billion.*

Of Mohammedan angels in the lowest heavens, as wanderers on the earth, there are this day more than two billion.

Of Jewish angels in the lowest heavens, as wanderers on the earth, there are this day more than thirty million.

And of other angels, idolatrous and otherwise, even on the earth, more than twelve billion.

Some of the wandering angels have entered the first resurrection and have begun to live with others:

And of all these angels not one is above grade five, in the first resurrection.

Why are there so many spirits bound to the earth? Not one of these angels is above grade five! They have developed only so far as to care five percent for others and ninety-five percent for themselves. Their religions failed to uplift them beyond a self-centered existence, and these spirits failed to grow beyond their selfish concerns. The result is that the spiritual environment on the earth is thick with ignorant, lost souls. These spirits wander around and inhabit the churches, homes, shops, bars, restaurants, and wherever there are humans. They are bound and lost.

This means that the chances of having an interaction with earthbound spirits are very high. Most mortals are influenced by the thoughts and feelings of the earthbound angels. These lost souls play back their own perspectives and prejudices on the people around them. In addition to the above numbers of earthbound souls, there are:

Of grade one, there are hundreds of millions of angels strolling about on the earth, crying out: I want to go to Brahma, I want to go to Buddha, I want to go to Jesus, I want to go to Kriste.

And I send my hosts of high-raised angels to them, saying: Come to the kingdoms of Jehovih, and be clothed and fed, and learn to clothe and feed others, for this is the way of resurrection.

But they will not believe, but turn away in stubbornness of heart, even as you of the earth, saying: No, I will rise only by prayers and confessions. I want to be changed in a moment, in the twinkling of an eye, and rise and sit on the right hand of God.

And there are hundreds of millions who, being dead, know nothing; but, through belief in a judgment day, went to sleep and are waiting for the trumpet of Gabriel to call them forth.

And I send my exalted ones to them to wake them up, and call them up; but they are drunk with their faith, and they relapse again and again, for years and years, for hundreds of years!

Fulfilling Creator's mandate, that whatever is bound on earth will be bound in heaven.

The lowest of the earthbound angels are called *drujas* and they are below grade one. These are the real troublemakers, demons or dark spirits:

But of such as are below grade one, there are more than six thousand million, which comprise such angels that know nothing more than babes, though for the most part they were full grown adults as to earth-life.

Some are fetals, some engrafters (professional re-incarnators),who dwell with one mortal during his lifetime, and then engraft themselves on another mortal during his lifetime, and so on, calling themselves reincarnated, and in fact knowing no other heavens, being disbelievers in the All Person and in my exalted kingdoms.

Such as are below grade one, I have classed this day as drujas, because they have not left the earth and entered the first resurrection.

What will become of these earthbound angels? How will they evolve beyond the earth? First their earthly anchor must be broken:

> *Know, O Man that all cities built by men, sooner or later, fall into destruction. And, in time, all holiness passes away from there; and, when your God abandons that city for a day, taking away his holy angels, the people fall into anarchy, or run with brands of fire and burn down the city.*

> *And the hundreds of millions of drujas lose their anchorage on the earth, and your God and his exalted ones march them away.*

Where does an earthbound spirit go when they are "marched away" from the earth? The higher angels take them to spirit hospitals to be healed and taught how to live in concert with the Creator. They are then assigned to the plateau or heaven most suited for them. Sometimes there are new plateaus created for them.

The Creator inspired the prophets of the major religions to teach Man to know the Creator and to live in harmony with the Creator. The basic laws that were given to all religions were sufficient to uplift humanity, but we were still too weak to take responsibility for our own actions. We fell to worshiping the prophets and looking to them to save us.

It was never intended for Man to worship the messengers, but rather to live the message.

Now the earth reaps the harvest of Man's ignorance, and we mortals are left to navigate through a chaotic environment of ignorance and fear. How can we do it? We can learn to live beyond the negative influences of this world that bind us and learn to living in harmony with the Creator. As we grow spiritually, we will attract spiritual companions who are not earthbound and who wish to help the earth become free of the bondage of ignorance:

Hear the words of your God, O Man, and be wise in your judgment: He who created you alive gave to you of His Own Being. Be steadfast to Him, and you will not err, but rather eliminate yourself from the chance of error. He alone is unmistakably your sure foundation, in whom you will not be tripped up.

Sufficient to you and your resurrection is your Creator. Wherefore, in your soul you will abjure all Gods and Lords and Saviors. Neither will you try to exalt His name by adding to it any name in the shape and figure of Man, nor by any one of woman born.

Seek to attain to His voice in all things, and to obey Him for righteousness sake. Be not stubborn in your conceit.

In your singleness of purpose you will be ministered to by the spirits of the first resurrection; but as you unite yourself in a brotherhood on earth, in the name of Creator, so will you be ministered to by the light of my second resurrection.

In order to rise above the failings of this world and establish a lasting governments or brotherhood/sisterhoods on earth we have to raise our consciousness above separation:

And all societies and constitutions and by-laws founded by people, not capable of the second resurrection, will fail. But whoever establishes in the second resurrection, which is the abnegation of self to serve Creator, will not fail.

A Call to the Jewish People - Chapter V

Here is a specific call to the Jewish people to come back to their original relationship with the Creator. The Jewish people have had a great history of being strong Faithists:

> And you will forsake the ways of the world, and go, and live after the manner of your forefathers, in colonies, without kings or rulers; serving none, but Creator. And your people will hold all things in common, being neither rich nor poor, master nor servant.

> And you will call out to the idolater, saying: Come into my house and be one with me. Behold, there is but one Creator; you are my brother. And it will come to pass to you, O Israel, the way of your people will be open, and they will be delivered out of the bound kingdoms of the east.

The Grades of Angels and Mortals - Chapter VI

Each person on earth and every angel or discarnate soul is graded by how much they are for themselves and how much they care for others. This grade represents the evolution of one's consciousness:

> He that serves himself one-half, and serves others one-half, will stand at grade fifty.
> He that serves himself three-quarters, and others one quarter, will stand at grade twenty-five.
> He that serves himself one-quarter, and others three-quarters, will stand at grade seventy-five.
> He that serves himself only, will stand at grade one.
> He that serves others wholly, will stand at grade ninety-nine.

How we treat ourselves, our fellow human beings and all life on earth will be the sum total of our spiritual grade when we leave our mortal body. Our spiritual grade determines where we go when we pass from mortal life into spiritual life. We go to the plateau that is best suited for our continued evolution.

There are angels who are lost in the darkness of their ignorance:

> *But there are some (angels) who are below the grades; who seek to do evil; who seek to make others unhappy; who delight in crime and pollution.*

> *These angels, if mortal, will be called druks, and if spirits, will be called drujas.*

What does it mean to serve one's self? Are we not supposed to take care of ourselves as well as others?

Nosce te ipsum

> *To serve one's self is to work for one's self; to strive for one's self, to think of one's own self, as to what will profit one's own self only.*

Service to others is the path of evolution for our soul and the highest service is to uplift and inspire others:

good

> *To serve others, is to do good to others;*
> *to help them;*
> *to teach them;*
> *to give them joy and comfort.*
> *This is the service of Creator.*

The angels of the higher heavens understand good works done to others, but their own evolution is not complete until they learn how to uplift others:

> *But good works alone are not sufficient to attain the highest grades, for they require knowledge and the capacity to unfold others.*

To accomplish which, those of the higher grades will often return to the lower, and learn to lift them up. For this is that which calls the ethereans in the times of resurrections.

The higher angels form lines of light from the second resurrection to the first resurrection and find ways to uplift those angels. Some of these lines of light extend to earth where the higher angels learn to uplift the mortals who have come together in service to others. The etherean Gods continue their evolution by going to planets like the earth and helping them through their evolution.

Where Do We Go When We Die? – Chapter VII

What can we expect when the physical body dies and the spirit moves into the next world? Who will we be? To what place will we go? It all depends on how we have lived our lives. All the outer trappings of the earth mean nothing in the spiritual worlds. It is the condition of one's heart and soul that determine who we are and to what place in the spiritual realms is best suited for us:

> *A Man may be wise as to books and philosophy and mathematics and poetry and great learning, and yet be low in grade as to spirit.*

> *A Man may know little of all such knowledge, and may be poor withal, but by hardship and experience, developed in sympathy and good works done to others, and be high in grade as to spirit.*

The same rules of existence in the spiritual worlds or heavens apply to the angels who manifest through mortals:

> *So also may it be with spirits that manifest through you as great orators, who stand even in the lowest grade in heaven.*

Who is it that is going to judge our behavior and our place in the heavens? It is we who will judge ourselves according to the knowledge of our soul:

You have the scales in your own hands, and will, sooner or later, weigh yourself justly, and take your place, even as you have prepared yourself.

Do not flatter yourself that you can cheat heaven, or change its ways.

Do not hide yourself behind doctrines, or behind the promises of Gods or Saviors.

Old things are done away, and none of these things will help you on earth or in heaven.

Be you king or queen or judge or servant, the same judgment will stand upon all.

Think about what it would be like without any physical possessions or even our body. Imagine being without social standing. Who would we be? What would we be like? In essence, who are we really, right now?

When the garment is gone, and the diadem and riches and the flesh withal, consider you the grade of your spirit and the bondage upon you. You will take that for which you have fitted yourself, according to what you have done.

Charity - Chapter VIII

What does it mean to grow spiritually? How do we develop our spirit? How do we help each other?

For in whatsoever you give, you will consider, first, the lowest of the low, whether they have bread to eat and a place to sleep; and the sick, whether they have attendance and good provision.

Those with the greatest need come first.

What is charity and true giving? We are asked to give according to our capacity:

> *For your resurrection depends not on the quantity you give, but as to whether you give according to what you have. Of which matter you will judge yourself. For he who gives a penny may be raised up more by so doing, than he that gives ten times ten thousand.*

How do we help others without promoting their dependence?

> *The measure of righteousness of that man's behavior was not in giving what he had to the poor, but in the good and evil that came of it, being weighed, as to which outbalanced the other.*

> *And where he lowered the grade of them that received this money, or where he lowered a greater number than he raised, there his act of casting the money away was a judgment against him.*

> *He who gives, saying: Here, you beggar!, does a good corporeal act, but an evil spiritual act. He lifts up with one hand, but knocks down with the other. Such an act takes away from the grade of that man.*

Charity is not just to alleviate suffering but to eliminate the suffering. We are to come together and organize to uplift and teach and help those who are trapped in poverty and sickness:

> *Let your charity be to the sick and helpless, but be wise in directing the able-bodied to help themselves. For all charity tends to lower the self-respect of the receiver, and casts him lower in the grades in heaven.*

One of the challenges we face when being of service is to release concern for our personal merit:

> Consider not so much what you will do to raise your own grade, but what you can do to raise the grade of those within your reach. Remember, all men and women are your brothers and sisters, and you should labor to make them make themselves a glory to the Creator.

The Grades of Cities and Nations – Chapter IX

A person is graded according to their spiritual development, and so are cities and nations graded according to their actions. A person's grade is also influenced by the grade of the city and nation in which they live:

> Nevertheless, a multitude of people make a nation, with cities and hamlets. These are also graded by your God, according to the ascendancy or the decline of the whole.
>
> If a city, then the grades of all the people will be summed together on a scale of one hundred. And if a nation, then the grades of the cities and hamlets, and of people of isolation, will be summed together on a scale of a hundred.

Does the country you live in have standing armies? Is it engaged in war? What is the percentage of crime in the city where you live? What percentage of the residents lives in poverty? These are the questions to ask when trying to discern the grade of a city or a country:

> Consider your nation, O Man, one generation with another; and as the relative proportion of individual grades rise or fall, so will you determine whether your nation is ascending or falling in grade. Number its paupers and criminals as to increase or decrease.

It all comes down to the individual grade of the people in each town and city. This will determine the grade of a city or a nation:

> And if half the people are above grade fifty, and half below fifty, the grade of that people will be fifty. On the basis of individual grades, will be the grades of a city and of a nation

It is not the physical wealth of a nation or the strength of its army that makes it strong. Our forefathers knew this when they wrote on our money, "In God We Trust." The unseen rules the seen and the true strength of a city or a nation lies in the spiritual strength of the people:

> Consider not its wealth, nor its ships, nor its armies, nor its great buildings. These all together are only grade one, and are of no value as to the spiritual grade of its people.

> For the strength and life of your nation depend on its spiritual grade. Pursue this, and you will prophesy truly as to the growth or the downfall of a nation.

The Grade of Each Individual - Chapter X

We are graded according to our capacities. What are our abilities and our responsibilities? How many people do we affect? What kind of an example are we in terms of uplifting and helping others?

> Hear then, your responsibility and the extent of it, and consider the magnitude of your own grade on earth and in heaven, which is in proportion to the power and the distance of your reach.

> If your Creator gives you strength to carry four men on your back and you will carry but one, you will be one-quarter grade. But, if you carry the whole four, you will be full grade.

> One man has wherewithal to feed one person; another has sufficient for a thousand; and another for a hundred thousand. These are the distances

of the reach and power of these people, which is the extent beyond which nothing more can be exacted of them on earth or in heaven.

Is it fair to ask one person to do so much more than another? What about those who work harder and those who wait for a handout? *The Oahpse* gives us a clear definition of spiritual responsibility. It is about each individual and what they can do to help other people. This is what life is all about. It is not about rich or poor, which is a temporary state of being. It is about each individual's capacity to serve.

When we pass from this world into the next and continue our journey of existence, we take with us nothing but ourselves. What have we really accomplished with our lives? Did we help make the world a better place?

And your grade of responsibility in heaven will begin even in the same place you established it on the earth. Where you were short, you will labor; where you did fulfill, you will rejoice and be without compunctions.

These spiritual laws also apply to those in positions of power and authority:

Also will this rule be with the king and queen and emperor, and all rulers who have means and power; and the responsibility will extend to all the people of the kingdom or empire.

Nor will this responsibility be escaped by death; but the bondage in heaven will be according to the avoidance of the trust imposed.

What happens to all the people who were harmed by an unjust ruler?

But if such emperor's dominions be in declension instead of resurrection, then, on his entrance into heaven, he will be at the mercy of the spirits of his kingdom, who will be in wait for him, and he will not escape them.

The angels of the higher plateaus are responsible to help with the transition of those who have been wrongly treated on earth; otherwise a hell would be created from the anger and revenge of these people upon their onetime rulers:

> *Some other heavenly kingdom will deliver them; otherwise, they fall into anarchy and madness.*

Life continues in the next world. We are on an infinite journey of becoming. We do not need to go back to earth to right the wrongs or the shortcomings of our life. We continue working on our weaknesses and desires until we finish what we could not while we were on earth.

Discerning Spiritual Grades - Chapter XI

It seems that Eoih wants us to make the effort to strengthen ourselves, to overcome our weaknesses and our selfishness, and at the same time not become self-righteous or conceited:

> *All men profess to desire resurrection; they hope to ascend to exalted heavenly spheres. Yet, many will not even try to exalt themselves.*

Life is a school, and all of us have strengths and weaknesses. No one is perfect, yet. All that Creator asks of us is that we do our best and care for each other. God knows, we have plenty of chances to do that:

> *And there are others who constantly profess to have the higher light; but they go about tattling, and making evil remarks of their neighbors. Yet, many of these do good to others, giving to the helpless; and they are both rising and falling, in regard to their resurrection.*

> *The measure of the grade of such will be by weighing the whole behavior as to its result in the community where he lives. And this rule will apply, both on earth and in heaven, to all such people.*

We have a tendency to believe that what we do outwardly is the most important thing. When we reach out to help others and donate to the poor we are really doing a good thing. Our actions are good but if we go home and tell great stories about ourselves and have a tendency to lie about people and ourselves we will be unbalancing the good that we have done. The condition of one's spirit is the most important thing:

There are men who do great good to others, and are talented withal, but who are great liars; and much prone to exaggeration. So, that their good works are outbalanced by the shame of their tongues.

The grade of resurrection of such will not be modified or benefited but little by their good works. But they will be weighed as to such evil habits, whether it be increasing or decreasing; and the grade of such a person will be accordingly, and will come under the rank of spiritual disease. Because it will be entailed upon them into the es world, and shut them out from the grade which they manifested.

The Grades of New Born Souls – Chapter XII

Some people innately feel and know the Creator, while others have to work at understanding even the possibility of a Creator. Some are born with this knowing, and some are not, depending on their ancestral lineage and the consciousness of their parents at conception:

Who sees not Him, are weak in spirit; who sees Him in all things, and hears His voice in the leaves and in every herb, are strong in spirit.

This does not mean that one is 'better' than another for we will all reach the fullness of our potential in the life to come:

My heavens rest upon the earth; the place of the es'yan is in my keeping. And the places of the grades of my heavens have I adjusted, according to the inhabitants who live there.

I people the heavens of the earth with the spirits of the dead; according to their grade in their corporeal lives, so I arrange them. To provide them to everlasting resurrection, and make them to rejoice in their being. These are the labors of your God.

The Animal Heavens

Many people wonder about what happens to animals when they die. *Eoih's Voice in the Wind* states that animals do not have an immortal soul. They have a limited life after death in the animal heavens, which rest on the earth in grade one. Their life in the spiritual worlds is for our consolation:

For the beasts of the field and the birds and fowls of the air, and for many animals that are companions to Man, I made a place in heaven, where their spirits should survive for a season.

And I made the animal heaven to rest on the face of the lands of the earth even the same as the place of the es'yan (newly deceased person now in spirit) in grade one.

Remember, O Man, your Creator gave to every animal a season on the earth; but He limited them to a time to become extinct. Even so, and of like duration made I a heavenly period for the spirits of animals companionable to Man.

The Physical Order of the Heavens

The heavens of the earth are divided into plateaus and oceans, just as the earth is.

In large bodies, He placed the lands; in large bodies, He placed the oceans. Not in little hillocks of land and little puddles of water. Even larger than these are the divisions (plateaus) of the heavens of your God; the heavens of the earth are separated by atmospherean oceans.

This allows for a comfortable transition for the spirits of the newly dead and others evolving through the first resurrection. The heavens are like the earth only more rarified:

> *I fill not the air of the firmament with angels scattered about; but I give to them regions habitable and home-like. And I grade them suitable to the resurrection of the spirits of the dead.*

The velocity at which matter moves determines the difference in dimensions. The higher the vibration of a substance, the more rarified it is. The more rarified a substance, the more expanded the molecular structure of the form. As matter is rarified, it moves from one dimension to another, from one form into another. The physical body is not as rarified as the spiritual body. The physical forms of the earth move slower than those of the spiritual realms. It is difficult for people to see the next world because it is moving faster than the normal range of sight. The rarification of matter is accomplished by vortexia:

> *Consider the work of your Creator, and the knowledge and symbols He places before you. You hold up a lump of salt, and it is solid and of dimensions; but cast it into water and it is seen not, but dissolved and lost as to your perception.*
>
> *And you behold the earth, which has dimensions also; but the ethe, you see not. As water is to salt the solvent, so is ethe to corporeal things the solvent.*
>
> *By slow velocity holds the solid earth its form; yet, in ethe, external to the body of the earth, the swift velocity of corpor is magnified into dissolution. By vortices in ethe are these things accomplished.*

The dissolved matter or corpor of the earth exists in the next dimension and is the material used to create the plateaus or heavens of the earth:

> *In the atmosphere of the earth, there is sufficient corpor to make many worlds like this habitable earth. And this corpor, which is in solution*

(as to a mortal's eyes), floats in the firmament of the earth, in continents wide as the earth, and deep as the earth; and there are thousands of them.

And yet, O Man, these are but the atmospherean heavens. These are the dominions given into the keeping of your God. These are my kingdoms and my heavens for a season.

The location of the angels in the heavens is according to their grade. The majority of spirits live closest to the earth in the inorganic heavens on the earth. The higher the grade, or vibration, of a spirit, the further away from the earth they live:

Consider the habitations of the resurrections of the dead which are in the keeping of your God. Even as to the square of the distance away from the earth, so are the grades of my resurrections.

According to the exaltation of Man's soul, so will he inhabit the places I have made. According to his own soul's growth and development, so will he ascend in my kingdoms, outward away from the earth; grade to grade I adapted them.

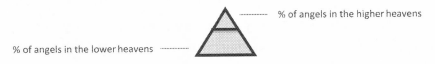

% of angels in the higher heavens

% of angels in the lower heavens

Distribution of the angels of atmospherea

Population of the Heavens

God Calls to Man to Awaken - Chapter XIII

O Man, to know the creations of your Creator and the things He has placed in your reach!

God calls out to Man to awaken and to listen to wisdom. We are so easily distracted by worldly things that we often forget about the divine presence all around us. Our concept of what 'should be' blinds us to what is:

Behold me, your God. I am your elder brother which He sent after you. Come, and learn the wisdom of your God.

You tarry in the grade; you are not aroused to know your Creator. You turn your back to me, and say: Behold, there is no God!

I beseech you, turnabout, and hear the wisdom of my words: I will teach you to know your Creator, to hear His voice and to see His hand. And you will rejoice in your life and teach your brethren to rejoice also.

Why does it matter if we know about spiritual life while we are alive? We can learn what we need to know later when we are in spirit. We need to develop our spirit while on earth in order to be able to function in the spiritual worlds and learning about our spirit and how to become spiritually strong will make the transition from earth life to spirit much easier. We are being called to awaken to our true potential as spiritual beings in a physical body. Our ability to create a world of peace and prosperity will require that we awaken to the fullness of ourselves while we are still mortal.

We were born in balance with spirit and matter, but the glamour of the world has made our physical awareness stronger than our spiritual awareness:

You have a corporeal body and a spiritual body: Hear me, and I will open your understanding. Your spirit has eyes and ears and judgment. Nevertheless, the beginning of your two parts was, at the same time, quickened into a one person, because of the presence of your Creator.

O Man of the earth would that your spirit and your corpor stood even in wisdom and power all the days of your life!

But you are so delighted in the earth that you have left your spirit unfed. And it stands within you as a spear of grass covered with a stone. And you see not spiritual things, nor hear the Unseen, for a stone lies upon your soul.

We have become highly intelligent in the physical world. We send rockets and telescopes into space. We bore holes into the core of the earth. We have developed bombs that can destroy the world. But poverty and crime and greed and suffering surround us.

Yet, you have great learning as to corporeal knowledge; and great vigor as to corporeal judgment. And you rate your neighbor a fool, because, in contradistinction to you, he hears and sees spiritually.

We are eternal beings and our true evolution is into spirit and away from a self-centered existence. Creator requires of us that we evolve into our true selves one way or another:

And your God weeps for you; because, in the time of your death, you will stand in heaven in grade one, even as the spirits of the beasts of the field.

Our spirit grows by searching to understand the Creator in all things, and by feeding it inspiring thoughts, seeking wisdom, helping others by bringing joy and relieving suffering.

We are responsible to develop our spirit. If we are not spiritually developed we will be as babies and will need assistance in the transition to spiritual life:

Your present knowledge will be void, and your vigor, only as a newborn child. And my angels who are wise and strong will take you about, in hada, the heavenly plateau that rests on the earth, and divert you with things closely related betwixt the two worlds, that you can be made to comprehend yourself and your Creator's work.

Food in Heaven

Our consciousness is accustomed to eating physical food. We need transition time to go from dense physical food to the essence of food, the spirit of food:

As your corpor was fed on corporeal substances, so, then, will your young spirit be fed on atmosphTherean substances, which your guardians will provide for you.

Consider the wisdom of your Creator, who sent me (God) to fetch you into places of delight. O that I could take you to the highest heavenly places! That you could stand before me and talk face to face!

But even as a newborn child is unsuited to feed on corn and nuts, your spirit is as a starveling in the high heavens.

And I take you to the nurseries where I have provided for you according to your weakness.

Spirit and Soul

What is the difference between the spirit and the soul? The soul is the presence of Jehovih within each person. The spirit is each person's individual manifestation of the divine. The physical body lives *within* the field of our soul and spirit. What we eat, what we think, and what we do, shapes our body and our spirit:

O that you had not contaminated your physical body by the flesh of the beast and the meat of His living creatures! This is as one of the stones that covers up your soul and blocks your way to the upper grades.

If we live on the flesh of animals while we are alive, we will be bound to the lower heavens in grade one until we have raised our vibration above the animal kingdom:

Your young spirit must remain within the atmosphere of the animal creation for a long season; like to like, have you fashioned your spirit to the flesh of your body.

Why does it matter what we eat? It is all Great Spirit. So are the poisonous creatures and plants. So are drugs, alcohol, and tobacco. We are here to learn and to discern what is good for us and what will bring happiness, peace, and harmony to the world.

It is all Creator and everything matters. The vibration of what we think, what we do, and what we eat all imprints itself upon our spirit. The spiritual essence of the food we eat is food for our spirit:

O Man of the earth, consider what you put into your mouth, for the atmosphere of that substance is the food of your spirit. And the habit of that will be entailed on your spirit for a long season after your mortal death.

If you have been a gross feeder on flesh, your spirit will seek to linger in the atmosphere of gross feeders still dwelling on the earth. The slaughterhouse and the cook-house and the eating-house will be the places of your spirit's resort.

We live in a world of free will, yes and no. If your will is to jump off a cliff and see what it is like to fly, the odds are that you will die. Your free will cannot transcend the workings of life itself. If we break Man's laws and we are caught, we will pay a price. If we break the laws of life we will pay a price. The price is not eternal damnation. It means that sooner or later we will have to come into balance with the All Light. If we do not cultivate our spirit here on earth, we will have to cultivate our spirit in the next world.

Strengthening Our Spirit

Our transition into spirit will be much more difficult if our spiritual body is weak, for we will not have the spiritual power to direct our lives in the next world:

> Consider your corporeal body as a ship in which your spirit is sailing across a wide sea of water. Better that your spirit learn to acquire strength while it has a corporeal body to ride in.
>
> After death, it floats in the direction you have shaped it. Neither have you power to go against the current.

How do we strengthen our spirit? How do we let go of things that do not result in lasting happiness for ourselves or anyone else?

> Stretch out your hand to your Creator and swear to Him you will conquer every passion that is unclean, and every habit not conducive to the purity of the growth of your spirit. This is the beginning of your resurrection, and you will be your own judge and master.
>
> Neither will you call out: God, God, exalt my soul! or O Lord, save me and raise me up!, until you have first begun to do something for yourself.

How will we know when we are growing stronger in spirit? We know. We feel goodness inside of ourselves, a strength and solidity in our character. We do things that we feel good about.

Most of the suffering and contention that exists on earth comes from the way we live:

O Man, would that you try to live in the ways that your God lives! You would put away the uncleanness of the body first, and the uncleanness of your spirit afterward. To seek for things that are pure and good, instead of criticisms and philosophies that rise up out of your contaminated flesh-house.

A major theme throughout *Eoih's Voice in the Wind* is that humanity has reached the time of maturity and we are responsible for ourselves and others. It is a time when we must uplift ourselves in order to become the fullness of who we are:

Whoever desires resurrection let him begin to resurrect himself.

How do we resurrect ourselves? We have to let go of the false self that has become the personality ruling our lives. The lesser self only serves itself. We have to embrace a new mindset, a new way of seeing the world and ourselves. Awakening doesn't come just from prayers or following a particle religion. We have to learn to listen to our soul and the soul of all things:

Such is the resurrection of the spirits of men. Do not wait
for a savior to save you; or depend on words or prayers;
or on listening to good sermons, flattering yourself, that
you have done well; but begin to save yourself.

This can be accomplished by purifying your flesh, by purifying your thoughts, and by the practice of good works done to others, with all your wisdom, love and strength. For through these only is there any resurrection for you, either in this world or the next.

The Foundations of Resurrection – Chapter XIV

There are many deciding factors in how we evolve. Two of the main ones are (1) the condition of our parents physically and spiritually before we are born, and (2) our ability to develop physically and spiritually during our lives:

> *Of the foundations of the resurrections of your God, there are two kinds; one, which deals with those already born, and the other, with such as are not yet born.*

Celibacy and Marriage

The earthly work of the angels who are in service to the Creator is to lift up mortals to become pure in spirit and in body. Purity comes by purifying the physical body with diet and lifestyle, and the spirit with noble thoughts and deeds:

> *For, after you have purified yourself as to flesh and spirit, two conditions are open to you, celibacy and marriage.*

> *Be wise as to the selection of your partner as to purity and righteousness. But be not deceived by such as eat not flesh merely, for the purification of the corporeal body is but half the matter. Look for one who is pure in spirit.*

These statements might seem a little outdated for the times we live in. Freedom and increased intelligence have changed our relationships. The call of spirit to live a holy life is often considered foolish, archaic, and stupid. Why should we make a commitment to each other for a lifetime when we can claim our right to change our minds whenever we want to?

Living for oneself has its own perspective and its own limitations. There are things in life that matter more than our fleeting desires or opinions. There are noble desires and there are self-centered desires. Freedom is complicated, and many cries for freedom are simply a license to fulfill individual desires or follow what a government or organization wants us to do. To see the highest path through it all is our challenge. If we want to help the world become a place of peace and prosperity then we must consider our responsibility in bringing new life into this world:

> *In likeness of the father and mother are all children born into the world; and every child is a new creation, quickened into life by the presence of the Creator, who is the All Life.*

There is marriage for personal or social gain, and there is marriage for love. The gift we give our children is who we are and how we live. Our children are the gifts we give the world. The angels who uplift humanity work to bring together mortals who are pure in spirit and in body to bring forth children that will help uplift the world:

> *If you are pure in flesh, your child will be pure; and, if you are pure in spirit, your child will be pure in spirit.*

> *If you are a flesh-eater, a drinker of strong drink, and a user of narcotics, your child will come forth with your contaminations upon it.*

> *Consider, then, what your grade will be, which will be according to your heirs, as to their grade in the place where they are born. As to whether you encumber the world with progeny lower in grade, or lift up the world by progeny of an exalted grade.*

How we live, what we think about, how we relate to other people and to all forms of life is very important to the evolution of ourselves and the whole world:

This has been revealed to you of old: Some are born of the beast and some are born of the spirit.

Which I declare to you, O Man is the interpretation of all the poverty and crime and war and licentiousness there is in the world.

This is the fountainhead, which your God would bring to the understanding of all people. But there are many, even hundreds of millions, that cannot be made to appreciate this. Nevertheless, the kingdom of peace and righteousness will not cover the earth over until this is understood by all men and women.

Original Sin

Be cautious in your proceedings.
He who created you alive gave you no sinful desires.

We are born pure of heart. We are imprinted with the consciousness of our parents, but we are still pure of heart. If we have no sinful desires does this mean that anything we desire is good? It is not that simple. We live in a world that constantly impresses itself upon us through the media, society, our friends and family, our inherited information and our own interpretation of what we experience. All these things add to us and often distort our pure desires, and thus the warning: *Be cautious in your proceedings*. Know who you are and what thoughts and desires are your own. Be aware that your true nature is without sin and will not encourage you to act in ways that are harmful to yourself or others.

The Abundance of Heaven - Chapter XV

Consider the inhabitants of the whole earth, and the number of billions brought into life every thirty-three years. Compute the numbers for a thousand years and for ten thousand years. And, yet, the earth is not

*full. And the heavens of the earth are yet even as if scarcely inhabited.
Thousands of plateaus are there, with no angels to dwell upon them.*

It is a great task for God to inspire the spirits of the dead to go away
from the earth and let go of their earthly desires so they can grow into
the higher dimensions. The earth is all they have ever known and for
some, all they have ever conceived of:

*But to induce the spirits of the dead to rise up from the earth, this
is the work and the glory of your God. To make them put away
earthly desires, to become pure and wise and strong and adapted to
the sublimated spheres, what an endless labor for your God and his
exalted angels.*

The dictionary describes sublimated as that which is purified and
exalted. The sublimated spheres probably refer to the etherean worlds.

The Percentage of Earthbound Souls

How does the population of the heavens affect us living on the earth?
It means that the spirits that live around us on the earth are very low in
grade. They are here because they are bound by their earthly desires.
These desires can be for family and friends, or for earthly food, alcohol,
drugs, money, power, etc. We are surrounded by lower influences from
the spiritual realms on earth. We must develop our connection to our
soul / Creator and strengthen our spirit in order to find peace and
happiness in this world:

*Consider, then, O Man, how sparse are the settlements in the upper
kingdoms of the earth's heavens, compared to the numbers in the lowest
grade. And remember, the percentage of inspiration that comes to you,
from this grade, which is doubly degraded in the cities and great capitals.*

The larger a city, the more drujas and earthbound souls there will be living in that city. If the unseen rules the seen, then one might understand why cities, in general, have a much greater problem with crime. When a city reaches a low grade, the higher angels who watch over that city remove themselves:

> *And, in time, all holiness passes away from there; and when your God abandons that city for a day, taking away his holy angels, the people fall into anarchy, or run with brands of fire, and burn down the city. And the hundreds of millions of drujas lose their anchorage on the earth, and your God and his exalted ones march them away.*

To lose their anchorage on the earth means that the greed, indulgence, and suffering that has fed the drujas is taken away when the cities are destroyed. They cannot stay because there is nothing to sustain them. All drujas are sustained by the energies of pain and suffering and indulgence. When a city is destroyed it is an opportunity for the angels to round up the drujas and take them where they can be rehabilitated so they will not pollute the earth anymore.

Like attracts like in the spiritual realms and if you seek earthly gain you will attract the spirits of those who are bound here by their earthly desires:

> *Do not call upon the spirits of the dead to come to you; but call on your Creator for wisdom and light and truth and purity; and, if it will be well for you, He will send to you such spirits as are best adapted to you for your resurrection.*

> *Whoever consults the spirits as to earthly things, or profit, or great undertakings, or marriage, or war, or riches, is already in the hands of drujas.*

Be fearful of the abundance of drujas about you; and search out your own imperfections and uncleanness and your passions, lest drujas fasten upon you in a way that you do not know.

It is not a bad thing to relate to the spiritual worlds. It is all about discretion and learning to understand what we attract and where to find true wisdom. Spiritual communion is one of the best ways to learn of the next world:

When you sit in communion with angels, do so reverently to your Creator; and the members of your circle will pray to Him, or sing songs of praise and glory to Him and His works.

Do not sit with such as do not have this reverence to Creator. And, when the angels appear and converse with you, remember that even the least of them have passed the bars of death.

Learning about the world of spirit is not a game; it is a reality that needs to be addressed with wisdom and respect.

Serving the Divine – Chapter XVI

O Man, weigh the words of your God, your elder brother, of tens of thousands of years' experience.

How do we live on earth in ways that attract goodness, create goodness and happiness, and bring fulfillment to others and ourselves?

Where your soul perceives a ray of light, follow it in truth and not in words merely. It has been said of old: You cannot serve both, God and self. And many go about preaching this, but they themselves, labor for self every day.

To serve your God is to work for others, especially the sick and helpless, and not for yourself. Your prayers and confessions to me are but the waste of your breath.

The path may not be easy, but it is the path that will purify and strengthen our spirit:

Suffer not yourself to be deceived by them whose trade is preaching and praying. They profess to be laboring for the spiritual Man; and, according to the number of their converts, who are also taught words and prayers and confessions, instead of works, so they are called great workers to the Lord.

But I say to you, all these are but the subterfuges of Satan, to palm off words for works. All such preachers and priests and converts are still tarrying in the mire of grade one.

Satan, in this context, is defined as the small selfish self that is afraid.

The preachers and teachers of all spiritual paths have a great responsibility to live what they teach. When they do, the world is richer and inspired. Gandhi, Mother Teresa, Rumi, Moses, Buddha, Joshua, and Confucius simply lived what they taught, and they changed the world for the better. The world today may offer us little encouragement to step away from selfishness, but it offers us great opportunity to serve others:

To remedy which, many practice serving themselves by their labor; but in Creator's service, their practice is by prayers and confessions: Words, words, words!

Saying: It is not possible in the present condition of society to do these things! Did your God limit you, saying: Do this, in the present condition of society? The way was open for another condition, but you sought not to find it. You would not give up yourself, and live in a brotherhood.

Under the name of liberty, you held fast to Satan and his haunts, saying: I am willing to serve the Creator, but I will not sacrifice my liberty.

This next quote is perhaps one of the most important to remember and accomplish. It is essential for spiritual growth:

Know then, O Man, that whoever would rise into my organic kingdoms in heaven, will teach himself the first lesson of liberty, which is to free himself from self.

It is not easy to live in service. Living in community with like-minded people strengthens our ability to let go of self and grow in spirit.

Here is a key to the upliftment and the enlightenment of the world:

I say to you. If you do not live in a brotherhood on earth, you will not soon find one in heaven.

But you will unite yourself with such as are compatible with you; with whom you will live equal in all things, and you can do to them as you would be done by, loving them as yourself, returning them good constantly.

Be willing to make any sacrifice of your own self's desires for the sake of founding the Father's kingdom on earth.

Here is a key to happiness and spiritual evolution:

For here lies the key of all resurrections, which is to labor for others and to inspire them to become one with the Creator and with one another.

Why is it so important to give up one's self? How do we give up ourselves, and what is left of us if we do? This is an issue of the smaller *self* versus the greater *Self*. The smaller self is focused on itself. It is turned inward and regards the outside world in terms of what it can get and how it can be protected against others. The greater Self is turned outward and views the world from a place of, "What can I give?" We have both the greater and the lesser selves within us. Learning to live beyond fear is one of the keys to moving into the greater Self. This does not mean we are never afraid; it means we move beyond fear when it arises.

What if we lived in an incredible, nurturing and kind universe composed of infinite supply? How would you live and act if that were the case?

The ability to trust in a benevolent universe that honors and loves you is essential. Trust in a benevolent universe is not about letting go of personal responsibility; we have to be responsible. It is about awakening to a new view of the world and our place in it. It is about the realization that we can open up and care for other people and be kind and reach out to help and have a wonderful life.

The greater Self looks at the behavior of others in a different way than the smaller self. If someone yells at us, the greater Self might feel sorry because it knows the person who yelled is having a difficult time. If someone steals your money, the greater Self understands that person has a great need or they wouldn't be stealing.

The greater Self lives in the immortal moment, knowing that we are divine beings having a human experience.

The Way to Peace on Earth - Chapter XVII

How do we as a civilization move forward away from crime and poverty and war? How do we make that leap of evolution that sets us free to be the fullness of who we are?

> *Remember the words of your God, O Man, and be reasonable in your understanding. Where ever you build a city, and it increases in*

inhabitants, it equally increases in pauperism and crime. Neither have you any doctrine under the sun to provide against this.

But I have now opened the book of knowledge before you. The place of my habitation and of the line of my light and of my holy angels I have made plain.

The way out of our dilemma is clear, give up our self-serving lives and uplift each other and care for each other. The way forward is not man against man. If we truly want peace and abundance for everyone we will have to change ourselves:

So I say at the gates of my exalted heavens, to the inhabitants of the earth: Only by knowledge and righteous works, done to one another, will you be able to endure the light of my kingdoms.

The strength and compassion we gain from service increases the light within us and increases our ability to take on more light. Service to others helps change our vibration to one of harmony with the resonant fields of the higher heavens. Purifying ourselves with a vegetarian diet, good and noble thoughts, and good works done for others will help uplift us and enable us to align with the light of the higher heavens.

Helping the Poor and the Sick

In this next quote, God explains how we can truly help the poor, the hungry, and the sick:

The healing of the sick may be compared to giving alms to the poor, and saying: Have I not done a good work?

I say to you, these things were of the past cycles.

They will now consider what will be done to prevent sickness. This is better than to heal.

They will now consider what will be done to prevent poverty.
This is better than giving to the poor.

When a new time of etherean lights comes to the earth the God/Goddess is like a new president in office. He removes the old staff and sets new agendas and laws that are appropriate for the times. These are great times, times of great change, and it looks like we are in for more changes. Everything is right for this planet to shift into a higher frequency of more light, and all life on earth must follow. It is time to help create heaven on earth. An increase in light is coming, and life, as we know it, is changing. We must change with it:

I have not come to heal and treat the diseased in flesh or spirit; or to re-establish any of the ancient doctrine or revelations. I am not a patcher-up of old garments.

I am not an apologizer for ancient revelations, nor have I anything in common with what is past.

Neither their doctrines, nor sacred books, nor their Gods, nor Lords, nor Saviors are anything before me.

I have not come to captivate the ignorant and unlearned, nor have I come to call sinners to repentance, nor to convert the debauchee, nor to convert the profane Man, nor to convert the harlot.

Sufficient have been other revelations to all these.
Nor have I come to say: Behold, this is my book! And there will be none other!

But, behold, I come to found Creator's kingdom on earth. I come to the wise and learned, and not to one person only; but to thousands.

Gods Challenge to Humanity – Chapter XVIII

God challenges the religious leaders of every church, every group, and every country in the world:

> Hear the words of your God, O priests and preachers and rab'bahs, and all of you that set yourselves up before men, professing to hold the key to salvation and the places of my resurrections in heaven.

> Listen to the words of your elder brother, God of these heavens and the earth; behold, I will set you in judgment over yourselves; and the powers of Creator within you will cry out for truth and justice.

> Take your chosen of the congregation of your church, and make manifest that which you preach. And prove that you have a good and sufficient doctrine for the salvation of your souls.

What does salvation mean? The dictionary says it is "the act of saving from harm or failure." Saving the soul from harm or failure seems like a good idea. If a spiritual path claims to know the way and the truth, they should be able to prove it. This challenge is given to all members of every religion: Understand the teachings enough to be able to live them daily.

One of the greatest challenges the angelic world's face is reaching the minds and hearts of humanity. It is difficult to communicate with people who cannot hear you and don't even know you exist. God says the condition of the body makes a difference in our ability to hear, see, and understand the spiritual worlds:

> You have not fulfilled the first law, which is to make clean your own corporeal bodies. Because you have stuffed yourselves with carnal food, my holy angels cannot approach you; neither can your understanding approach the place of my kingdoms.

If the oil and air filters on your car are really dirty from lack of maintenance, it will be difficult if not impossible for your car to go down the road, because the fuel and air can't get to the engine. You might have great intentions to reach your destination, but your car is stuck. Similarly, many people are stuck. They want inspiration; they seek the truth; and they believe in the Divine. But they have to rely on someone else to show them the way because they do not understand the first law. If we cannot understand the first law of purifying the flesh, how will we progress with purifying the soul?

How much less, then, have you purified your souls? Wherever you will not put away flesh, because you love flesh, even so will you not put away self-righteousness?

Because you shun the practice of labor, showing to the world, you love words, and the renown of men and caste, making preferences in your churches, having rich and poor, which is itself your condemnation.

For you should divide with one another; putting in practice your doctrines. What one of you has a congregation who has given up all, and who make themselves alike and like, rich and poor?

The time has come on earth when we must evolve beyond our separation and conceit. We must move beyond our present conscious limitations to embrace the possibility of a world that works for everyone and lives in peace. We have the means to feed the world. We have the means to stop fighting. We could create a world where everyone has a place to live and food to eat, and purpose to their lives. We can all start to live a little closer to this possibility, now.

God Gives a New Religion - Chapter XIX

Not another religion! *The Oahpse* teaches how to live our lives in concert with the divine so we can reach our highest potential on earth and in the heavens. This is not about establishing another church or organization. This all about how to live:

Do not flatter yourselves, that, because you wear fine cloth and you preach that you are not responsible also. Nor hope that when you become spirits, you will ascend suddenly into places of delight. You are marked by your God!

Your souls are written all over with your deeds and works and words; and you will see yourselves as in a mirror, and of your own accord shun my kingdoms of light. Because you have learned word, and practiced only in words, behold, I come in this day to command practice in works. Not for a pittance, but for all you have.

I have not come to destroy your religions; you have done that already. I come to give you a religion where all men can be as brethren.

Religion is defined as a set of beliefs concerning the cause, nature, and purpose of the universe. Humanity has long lived in a world in which religions are institutions against each other. These organizations have become so far removed from their original intentions that they take countries into war and destruction. Many people are repulsed by the word "religion." They say, "Don't talk to me about religion. I've been there and done that." Falling away from the old ways is good, but it doesn't mean there wasn't a divine seed in the beginning, even though they have failed us, just as we have failed them.

Many people are leaving the old religions and planting new seeds of spiritual awareness. It is time to cast off everything that holds humanity back from its evolution. The traditional religions hold much wisdom as well as limitations. Let us hope that we can still honor the universal wisdom that has been given us as we move into our future.

God has made it clear that prayers and praise are of no use to influence him. He wants action not words:

When you cannot purchase one another by flattery, how do you hope for the favor of the Almighty, by praise and prayers and flattery? Behold, the selfishness of Man has made the world like a house on fire! My little ones are in pain and suffocation. Go, then, quickly, to them, and provide a remedy. This is the new religion I give to you: Demanding sacrifice of you, and your congregations, of all you have, that is not in use and actual need.

The last sentence demanding all you have that is not in use and actual need is important in understanding how to proceed. If we give away all we have and can't take care of ourselves, we will become the poor we seek to help. Perhaps we will not be able to help, but only commiserate with the poor. This statement calls us to give up everything we do not need to sustain us and help others with what extra we have. Sustain us means voluntary simplicity. We don't need several cars and closest full cloths and big houses for one or two people. We need to minimize to what we really need and help others with their needs.

This is about actions, not words. Many people talk about solutions and problems, and some are reaching out to help as best they can. But many people just talk about it. Perhaps some people think that it is enough to speak out against injustice and then go back to living their lives. God says the Divine Presence is tired of all our talk and promises and ideas. Only action will solve the problems and bring balance back to the earth and the people:

Now, behold, I come in this era, not only to declare to you that the time of preaching is at an end, save where it is practiced in deed as it is spoken in word, but also to prophesy to you that many of you will give up your calling and preach no more.

And your temples and churches and meetinghouses will be turned into consultation chambers to find remedies against poverty, crime, and debauchery.

Judgment and Liberty - Chapter XX

We have fine-tuned our ability to judge things, including our friends, events, and possibilities. We need to learn how to clearly judge ourselves, even our very souls:

God said: There will be a day of judgment to you, O Man. Sooner or later, you will take the matter into your own hands, and you will look into your own soul to judge yourself. This is to all people; none can escape it.

Such is the judgment day. Let no Man complain against the judge; you will be your own judge

Benjamin Franklin practiced daily introspection. At the end of each day, he would review what he had accomplished and how he had acted. This is a wonderful way to keep track of what really matters:

But, whether you will judge yourself in this life, or wait till you are dead and risen in spirit, the matter is in your own hands. It would be better for you if you would sit in judgment of yourself every day of your life.

God describes spiritual growth and its attributes. The first sentence in the next quote is worthy of striving toward for the rest of our lives:

Your spirit grows by cultivation, which is by the practice of wisdom, truth, virtue, benevolence and affiliation to others.

We often feel an affinity to a spiritual path or a spiritual teacher. Different ways of teaching and saying things awaken different people. It is not wrong to be uplifted by a spiritual teaching or a spiritual leader:

Think not, that the soul grows by prayers or confessions to this God, or that God; for, in whatsoever God you firmly believe, him will you worship, for he is your choice.

Nor will any one prevent you in this your liberty. But, remember, the same rule holds to all in this day:

You will never see the God you worship, save, indeed, it be an idol, or an image of wood or stone or some corporeal substance.

Nevertheless, if you worship a God, or Lord, let it be as a figure to you to cast your eyes into your own soul, to purify yourself in the sight of your Creator, whom you cannot doubt. In such respect, it is no sin for you to worship any good ideal, whom you will emulate in your behavior.

Spiritual Deception

The laws of attraction between the physical world and the spiritual worlds are exacting. We often attract to ourselves beings or events that we do not want because we do not understand these laws:

This also will you prove: That, whosoever of the ancients was great, or whatever Gods were well known that you set your soul on to love, behold, familiar spirits will come to you to deceive you, professing to be that ancient or that God.

We are supposed to keep our focus on the Great Spirit, the Creator of all things, and not on anyone born of the earth. It is good to emulate the great people of this world, and that includes the prophets, but we are to worship only the Creator. God warns Man that he can be deceived in the next world if he has given his heart to worship a person born on earth. The lower spirits often appear as a famous person or prophet in an attempt to deceive and use an unaware person. They will even pretend to be the Creator:

And, when you are dead, and your soul rises from the dead, behold, some deceiving spirit will come to you to use you; neither will you discover for a long season that you have been the dupe and slave of an unscrupulous master.

We are like children and will be easily deceived by the lower spirits, in death as well as in life. We can learn to know the difference between the inspirations of deceiving spirits and the presence of the Creator. One of the keys is that we will never see the Creator as we would see a person, for He is All That Is, beyond all form and within all form:

Think not that great wisdom comes suddenly by dying; in your early entrance into the es world, you will be easily deceived.

For which reason you should school yourself every day of your life, that your Creator only is your God and that Him you will never see as you see a Man or an angel; but that Him also you can see every day in the glory of His works.

How do we judge ourselves and our actions? How do we know what is truly right or wrong? There are so many different opinions from so many different people. How do we know?

Now, therefore, when you judge yourself, to determine the balance of your good and evil deeds, and your good and evil thoughts, let your Creator stand as the light of your soul, and, through Him, judge yourself, but not as to your worship, but as to your works.

This next quote is an empowering statement, for anyone who takes it to heart. We are responsible only to the Creator:

Neither will you judge yourself by any God, or Lord, or Savior, or by any idol or by any man or woman; for you stand yourself second to Creator in your attributes. It behooves you to make a God of yourself, in your behavior and in your words and deeds.

Neither will you judge yourself by any sacred book, or any bible in the entire world; nor by the words within them purporting to be my words, or the words of any God, Lord, or Savior.

Not only are we to judge ourselves, we are also not bound by any word that is written or printed in any book or sacred writing, including this one:

Neither will you bind yourself by them, or judge yourself by anything that is written or printed in them.

But, behold, I declare a greater glory and judge to you in place of this, which is Creator, your Creator. By Him and through Him will you judge, and be judged.

Consider the ideas of others, but rely only on the Creator. All the books and religions and ideals are wonderful to inspire us and sometimes mislead us. These books and organizations have been handed down to us by other people. The Creator has spoken through God to many people, and they have written down what they gleaned, but this information comes to us indirectly and often through centuries of interpretations. These writings do not come directly to us. If they inspire us, great, if they don't, fine. Each of us is to find our way directly to the source and to join with others of like mind.

We are the children of the Creator and can converse directly with the Creator. As we learn to speak directly with the Creator, we will be able to understand more clearly what is right for each of us, according to our direct inspiration.

Our Responsibility - Chapter XXI

Now that humanity has come of age, our relationship to God and life is different. We are evolving, and with our growing consciousness come responsibility:

Now, that you have attained to comprehensive judgment, Creator has inspired you to liberty, and to think for yourself, and to consider what is best for you. And your God comes not now as a dictator, but as your elder brother, with ample experience.

And I say to you, after the manner of your professors in the college to their graduated classes: Behold, you are free; go your way, and no longer hope to hold your God accountable for your behavior.

Now that humanity has come of age, we are even more responsible for our actions. We are charged with being completely accountable:

For, with your freedom, you also have responsibility. Think not, because I emancipate you from the God and Lords and Saviors of the ancients; and from the bibles and sacred books of the ancients; and from the ancient commandments and injunctions, that, as a consequence, you are not bound in fidelity to your Creator.

To be bound in fidelity is to stay loyal to the Creator and to know that even though we are no longer bound by the past and the doctrines of the past, there has always been a higher purpose to morality, nobility, and the recognition of the sacred. But now we must find this truth for ourselves so our fidelity to the Creator will be impregnable. The Creator charges us with the work of understanding the sacred:

So, that your fidelity to your Creator and to your fellow Man, in righteousness, love and good works, will be the most sacred study of your life.

And your example from day to day will be a perpetual register of your accountability; verily will you be a living sermon before men and before Creator.

God warns us to be careful of our actions when we are set free from the constraints of religions and social morays:

157

Beware, O Man, for this rule applies to all the generations of men:
That, by sudden emancipation from an old condition, Man runs into
another extreme, from which spring libertinism and licentiousness.

What are libertinism and licentiousness? The dictionary describes a libertine as someone who indulges in pleasures that are considered immoral and who has sexual relationships with many people. Licentiousness is defined as pursuing desires aggressively and selfishly, unchecked by morality, especially in sexual matters.

We have been set free and we are now swinging to the opposite side of the pendulum with regards to our integrity, morality, and spiritual growth. We are free to do as we wish. How else will we ever grow up and stop using and destroying each other? We have to come to a place where we understand that our relationships are sacred, and that each person is sacred. We have to learn for ourselves that our actions matter and have consequence on earth and in the next life.

Living without morality or integrity, or an awareness of the sacredness of life, will only bring pain, suffering, and regret. As we learn to judge ourselves we must also be aware of the conditions of the state and how best we can serve at that level.

More on Earthbound Souls

During this time on earth, the veils between the worlds have been opened and the spirits that dwell near or on the earth have become interactive with mortals. Everyone sees life differently, according to his or her experiences, and so it is within the spiritual realms:

Because I have opened the heavens, the spirits of the dead return to
you and commune in your household; flatter not yourself that the whole
of the Father's kingdoms are revealed to you, and that the angels who
converse with you can make plain the dominions of the higher heavens.

Earthbound spirits have a limited perspective of the angelic realms, and they do not realize many of the laws of progression in the spiritual worlds. They have not experienced the heavens, so they do not know they exist:

> *Many of these will return to you, saying: There is no hell, no Satan, no God, or Lord, nor anything in this world to make you afraid. For, of a truth, the hell they looked for, they did not find; nor did they find a God, or Lord, or Savior, such as they had hoped to find. And, for this reason, such angels are jubilant for the time being.*

God gives us fifteen commandments to live by in order to become one with the Creator and all life:

- *To love the Creator above all else*
- *And your neighbor as yourself*
- *Sell all you have, and give to the poor*
- *Return good for evil*
- *Do good to others, with all your wisdom and strength*
- *Abnegate (give up) self in all respects;*
- *Making yourself a servant to your Creator*
- *Owning or possessing nothing under the sun*
- *And look into your soul, to judge yourself constantly, to discover where and how you will do the most good*
- *Complaining not against Creator for anything that happens*
- *Making your neighbor rejoice in you*
- *Making yourself affiliate*
- *Without self-righteousness above any one*
- *Being a producer of something good*
- *And learn to rejoice in your own life, with singing and dancing and with a jovial heart, paying due respect to rites and ceremonies, that all things may be orderly before Creator.*

> *Remember the words of your God, O Man, when angels or men advise you against these commandments, they have little to offer you that will promote the harmony of the state. Consider, therefore,*

that whatever promotes the greatest harmony and wisdom within the state has also been discovered and is in practice in the higher heavens.

Thy Kingdom Come - Chapter XXII

God said: I have heard your prayer, O Man: Your kingdom come on earth, as it is in heaven.

Have you considered your words? And are you prepared for it? Have you fulfilled the commandments? And do you love your neighbor as yourself? And have you done to the least as you desire your Creator to do to you?

These are good questions, but they are a little frightening. Most of us are far removed from what it really means and what it really takes to create heaven on earth. We read inspiring words and hold good thoughts, and we dream of a better world. We donate to good causes, and we give time to organizations, but what would we do if we were asked to live as Joshua lived, or Buddha, or Chine, or Zarathustra, or the higher angels? Do we have the strength, the trust, and the knowing that it is possible to really live what these teachers taught and still survive?

Here is one of the requirements:

I demand of you, that you have no favorite doctrine above your neighbor; And that you are a servant to no God, or Lord, or Savior, or church, unacceptable to any person in the entire world. But, that you serve Creator with all your wisdom and strength by doing good to your fellow Man with all your might.

The new religion of the world will be all about helping each other. I suspect that the Creator is tired of our quarreling over who is right and who is wrong. What a great solution for humanity: Stop fighting about it and live it.

We have debates about righteous war, self-defense, and all the other reasons we embrace for fighting with each other. We live on a planet full of siblings, all quarreling over their toys and territories. The Father stands up and says, "Enough! Give it all up! Grow up! Now!"

> *I demand of you, that you will give up your army and navy. Are you prepared to say: To who strikes me on one cheek, I turn the other to be struck also?*
>
> *Is your faith still more in weapons of death than in the Voice of Everlasting Life?*
>
> *Do you hold your army and navy higher and depend on them more than Creator?*
>
> *Are you willing to sacrifice your time and money and self-interest for sake of Creator's kingdom?*
>
> *Use your judgment, O Man. Since the time of the ancients till now, the only progress towards the Father's kingdom has been through sacrifice. What less can you expect?*

Many of us are doing our best to bring peace, justice, and happiness to others, but humanity still fights and kills and steals. God says the world is stuck in its ways, and that we should remove ourselves from the cities and move into communities dedicated to the Creator in order to create a new world:

> *But you will go away; and, behold, I will go with you, and with your neighbor, and show you how to build even as a kingdom in heaven.*

The New Earth - Chapter XXIII

God speaks about why the new earth cannot grow within the old structures:

> *I have not come to repeat former judgments against whom all people understand to be sinful; for, behold, I gave governments into the hands of Man, to deal with these things themselves.*
>
> *But I have come to the leaders of men; to kings, queens, emperors and presidents; and to philosophers and men of learning, priests, rab'bahs, cardinals and popes; and to merchants, bankers, manufacturers, farmers, shippers, and hucksters. Such as pass unscathed before the laws and government of Man, and are reckoned passably wise and good before the world.*

God is asking all of us and especially those who are responsible to groups of people, to move to the next level of consciousness:

> *Therefore, O Man, hear the judgment of your God against them: They are not united and affiliated as brothers.*
>
> *But the best of all of them are as so many individual entities pulling in different ways, every one for himself.*
>
> *The Brahmins are not communal; the Ka'yuans are not communal; neither are the Buddhists, nor the Kriste'yans, nor the Mohammedans; neither the philosophers, priests, merchants, nor any one people in the entire world.*

The solution seems to be community and communal living. It's about working together:

> *Now, hear me, O Man, and consider the wisdom of your God: Satan is wiser than any of these I have named. For Satan has made armies of soldiers communal. He has discovered the power of affiliation and discipline.*

Behold, a thousand soldiers are more efficient than ten thousand men, unorganized.

The Bondage of Earth

The ways we live on earth will dictate where we will begin in the spirit world. At this time on earth many of the mortals who die are earthbound. They have no idea of the organization of the heavens or the worlds around them:

> *Now, behold, I said to you, in the olden times, try the spirits, and see, if they be of God. For the angels who wander about on the earth know not my kingdoms, and they deny me, and deny all order and system and discipline in heaven and earth.*
>
> *And each and all such angels, coming to mortals, do so on their own account, assuming any form and name they may find acceptable to men. Such angels have not yet entered the first resurrection; nor do they belong to any disciplined kingdom in heaven.*
>
> *And all mortals, such as I have named to you as the best and highest of mortals, enter the es world (after death), only into the inorganic regions of heaven.*

As we evolve our spirit expands to take on more light. Then we are able to endure the higher frequencies of the next dimension. The discussion about good verses not so good, self verses selfless, and helping others or being self-oriented is about raising our vibration, or frequency, to higher levels of consciousness. It is all about our spiritual evolution. If we are not able to let go of a self-oriented life, we will be bound to that which we desire until we grow beyond our isolation:

> *Therefore, after death, they remain, for the most part, in their former places: The merchant in his counting-house, the banker in his bank, the shipper in his place, the philosopher in his place, the pope in his*

place, the king in his, the farmer in his. Neither have they the power or wisdom to go to any other place, or to stroll about.

They are like one that has lost his master. Neither will they affiliate with other angels, but in stubbornness and moroseness, they persist in working out an individual identity until they are broken down in sorrow and darkness, which may be in a few years, or it may be hundreds of years. And, then, my holy ones come to them, and carry them away to my es'yan schools.

The Angels Who Help Mortals? - Chapter XXIV

How do we know what kind of angels are influencing us? How do we know if the inspiration we receive is good or misleading?

> *God said: One rule have I given to all people, by which it may be known what kind of angels' minister to them; that rule is a mortal's own manifestations and behavior.*

We will know by how we are inspired, to self or to service.

> *Whoever manifests serving himself chiefly has little light*
> *from my organic kingdoms; but whoever serves Creator*
> *by laboring for others, with all his wisdom and strength,*
> *is attended by the light of my organic kingdoms.*

Many people talk these days about being guided by a spirit, an angel, an ascended master, Jesus or Buddha, or a famous person. Maybe they are and maybe they aren't. "By their fruits you shall know them" is a familiar phrase, and it is true when trying to discern where a person's inspiration comes from.

For the most part, a single spirit who manifests to a mortal is an earthbound soul living close to the earth, where they mostly serve themselves. They have not become communal or in service to the Creator. Opinions or inspiration may have merit, but not because it came from a spirit or angel. We are to judge all things based on what is said, not on who said it.

The religious teachings of old were given to help the people of those times and lead humanity forward. The old teachings were to help them understand how the angels live so they would be prepared when we cross over into spirit and not become earthbound:

> *When you were taught of old to say: May your kingdom come on earth as it is in heaven, it was instruction given to you to lead you in the method of my dominions.*

Earthbound souls or wandering spirits have not joined the organized heavens of the first resurrection. They wander about living independently and for the most part they are ignorant of the existence of the first resurrection:

> *As to wandering spirits, they have not yet entered the first resurrection; but, such as have enlisted in my organic kingdoms, are called es'eans, whilst learning the rites and discipline, and are said to be in the first resurrection. And such as have become organic workers are in the second resurrection, and this is a kingdom of heaven.*

> *This rule is also uniform in all my heavenly kingdoms: After entrance into the first resurrection, none of the angels return as individuals to commune with mortals, except as I have mentioned, or save when especially commissioned by me or my Lords.*

The first resurrection has its rules and discipline to help the spirits grow away from the earth so they will not be bound by the desires and activities of the world.

The Second Resurrection - Chapter XXV

The spiritual worlds are organized and dedicated to the upliftment of humanity. They keep track of everyone. We on earth are not alone:

> God said: In the cities and country places, I have innumerable Lords, apportioned to districts and to the mortals and angels who abide there. And my Lords know the rates and grades of their people, their occupations, their aspirations, and their labor, their behavior, private and public.

Communal Brotherhoods

In an effort to assist humanity to uplift itself, the higher angelic realms work to educate us about the laws of cause and effect and how we must live in order to receive more assistance from the higher angelic realms:

> And I further said to my Lords: Man has prayed, saying: Your kingdom come on earth as it is in heaven. Now, this I give to you: That where men abnegate self and affiliate into a communal brotherhood after the manner of my heavenly kingdoms, then will you affiliate my organic angels with such mortals and make them one with my second resurrections.

This means not only access to greater assistance and wisdom, but also greater protection from deceiving spirits:

> And you will surround such communal brotherhoods with the light of my kingdoms, thereby controlling the angelic intercourse with mortals, so that drujas and vampire spirits cannot molest them.

Why do we need protection from these lower spirits? Lower spirits tend to latch onto mortals and interfere in their lives. They often cause arguments, dissension, and anger. Some even delight in causing chaos and suffering.

How does a person who is not living in a communal setting that attracts the higher angels, protect themselves from the lower spirits? Watch where you go and the kinds of people you are with. Lower spirits are attracted to selfish people, alcohol, drugs, fighting, stealing, cruelty, greed, domination, and war.

How do we know whether a lower or higher spirit is inspiring us?

> *Neither has it ever happened on the earth with any individual person, raised up by me or my Lords for a specific work, like Moses, or Ka'yu, or Sakaya, or any other, that they knew of or boasted of any special angel over them; but all of them experienced the light, which was as a pillar of fire.*

If a spirit shows itself to us, they are likely from the realms closest to the earth, the inorganic heavens, and the place of the earthbound souls. If we receive inspiration from a voice that does not declare itself with a name, then it could be our higher self, our guardian angel, or an earthbound soul. Angels of the first resurrection are not usually allowed to return to the earth so it would not be from there. Only if we live our lives in concert with the second heavens will the angels of the second resurrection be able to assist us.

Second resurrection angels are at least fifty percent for others. They have grown into a greater affiliation and dedication in service to Eoih. When groups of people come together in service to the Creator, the angels of the higher heavens can link with them to assist and inspire them.

This new era on earth, which has been heralded by so many, is indeed an amazing time. Just look at science. The *Through the Wormhole* series on The Science Channel has declared the possibility that because everything in the universe is linked to everything else, and all is alive and moving, it is possible that what we call *God* or *Creator* is the universe itself. The last one hundred years have been a time of accelerated growth in consciousness for both spirituality and science:

> *O Man, I declare to you that the Father's kingdom is now being founded on earth, and the mortal manifestation of this is near at hand.*

> *But it will not come in this era, as in the past, through any one great leader; but it will appear as a spontaneous light, permeating the souls of thousands and they will come forth establishing Creator in truth and fullness.*

God Judges the Ascetic - Chapters XXVI

God speaks out against the life of the ascetic. He speaks against the rites and ceremonies, the rules and punishments that are used to imprison the mind. Inquisitors who inflict petty punishments in order to change human behavior are actually preparing their followers for bondage in the next dimension:

> *For the same rule holds on earth and in heaven as regards the bondage of the mind. If, by imposing rites and ceremonies, and by the strategies and cunning of mortal priests, they can be captured on earth, even so can they be retained in bondage in heaven.*

> *And it happens with them, that even as they honestly believe they are right on earth, so will they persist they are right in heaven, even willingly submitting to cruelty and torture in order to prove their fidelity.*

Some people who pursue a religious life do so to enlighten themselves, not for the service of others. Some say that a person cannot serve or help others until they have enlightened themselves. There would not be many people available to help others in this case:

> *Be considerate, O Man, of the words of your God. He who created you gave to you one star of light by which you may determine truth and wisdom. Whatever doctrine shows self as the chief consideration, even if it be for obtaining wisdom or supposed purity for self's sake, is not of Creator.*

Again the theme of doing good works is presented, not just praying or talking about it, but in some way seeking to uplift humanity:

> *But you will weigh their prayers also, and you will estimate the value of them by what is accomplished.*

> *And you will prove whether their prayers provided harvests of wheat and corn, and food and clothing for the poor, and education for the unlearned, or any other thing that was good.*

God Judges Charities - Chapter XXVII

God speaks about charities. What is the wisest way to help others? How do we help make the world a better place? How do we assist those who cannot help themselves?

> *Where you apply charity and it is not self-sustaining, judgment is rendered against you.*

> *You may feed three drunkards' families, and flatter yourself you have done a worthy charity, but if you have not done that which will make them no longer in need of charity, you have done little.*

> *Another man may not feed them, but he may reform them and put them in the way to be self-sustaining. Such a man will have done a hundred-fold greater charity.*

How to best serve is an age-old question. The highest way to serve is to teach people to take care of themselves. Until this can be accomplished, we can still help where we can, with the goal toward helping people help themselves:

> *Yet, you will avoid going to the other extreme, doing nothing, which is worst of all. But you will go to the root of the matter; your charity will be directed to prevent the causes of such ill-fortunes.*

Good Charity - Chapter XXVIII

How do we create a solution for the many problems people have? How can one person make a difference?

> *It has been said: Sell all you have and give it to the poor; but I say to you, you will not do this. Though that opened the way to salvation in the ancient days, it is not sufficient in this day.*
>
> *Neither will you hope that by giving to the poor you will escape condemnation. But you will go to the foundation of things, and go systematically. Your efforts will not be single-handed, but you will unite with others, and, together, you will provide a remedy against poverty.*

Many people have learned that it is better to save the children first. This is not to say that others do not need assistance, indeed they do, but the children are the future:

> *Remembering, it is wiser to accomplish with the young than with the aged. For the mature will be dead in a few years, and, in that day, those that are children will be mature.*
>
> *Better is it that you provide a way to ten fatherless children, than for forty people that are grown.*

Putting children in orphanages is better than leaving them on the streets, but what of teaching them how to take care of themselves and others?

> *For it is not sufficient that you feed and clothe little ones; but you will teach them a trade and occupations, and give them learning, so that when they are grown they can sustain themselves.*

> *But, even yet, your work is not the highest; but you will so provide them, that they will not only be self-supporting, but that they will be willing and capable of rescuing others, as they were rescued.*

When we find a way to serve humanity, the next step is to make sure it continues:

> *Therefore, let your charity be not for a year, nor for a hundred years; but be you the cornerstones, founding places on earth where will rest perpetually a system that will provide a new race, where poverty and crime and helplessness cannot enter*

Missionaries - Chapter XXIX

God constantly reminds us that life keeps changing, and what was good for Man before is no longer. In the past, Man was encouraged to travel the earth and preach about the doctrines of that time:

> *God said: In the olden time, I commanded you, saying: Go forth into all the world, preaching my doctrines, chief of which was: There is but One, even the I Am; Him will you love with all your heart and your mind and your soul, and love your neighbor as yourself, having faith in Creator through righteousness and good works.*

But mankind was not conscious enough to hold the concept of the Creator in all things. Mankind needed an image it could grasp and relate

to, and so people began to worship Lords and Saviors they could see
and understand:

> But it came to pass, in course of time, you forsook
> your Creator, setting up Lords and Saviors of your
> own, worshipping them instead of Creator.

As mankind fell further away from the teachings of the Creator,
domination and destruction replaced love, kindness, and compassion:

> And I measured the work of your hand in the places of your mission,
> and I found that you were impotent to establish good works.

> And, following in your path, where ever you had gone, thousands and
> millions of drujas followed you; and your people went with weapons of
> destruction, slaughtering those Creator had created alive, in order to
> establish your idol-God.

The Creator admonishes the missionaries of the fallen religions:

> Neither had you raised up any member, or members in all of them, that
> practiced even the first commandments.

The Creator judges against the major religions and their proselytizing:

> Do not flatter yourself that you have done a good work, because you have
> taught the ignorant to say: Brahma, Brahma!, or Buddha, Buddha!, or
> Lord, Lord!, or to sing anthems in praise of your idol-God.

The Responsibility of Power - Chapter XXX

What happens to those who have power on earth and use it to dominate or possess?

> *And when a king possesses himself of a new country, he not only receives its riches but its misfortunes also. The profits and losses are all his. And the sins of the people are his, and are henceforth upon his head.*

Our actions on earth follow us into the spiritual worlds, and we are responsible for whatever we possess:

> *Moreover, judgment will pursue that king into the es (spirit) world; and the subjects he took to himself on earth will be his in heaven to redeem, and provide for, and educate.*

Justice is universal but not always immediate. We are always responsible for our actions and especially our actions toward other people:

> *For every one whom the king causes to be slain in order to possess a new country, the king will meet out retribution until all his enemies do pardon and forgive him.*

Many people complain that life is not fair. What we often forget is that life is ongoing and immortality is forever. Earth life is a small piece of our existence. It is the beginning of our journey. What we put into motion continues until balance is achieved. What a person does on earth follows them into the next world:

> *And the same rules will apply to every king and queen and emperor, and every other ruler in all the world.*
>
> *The resurrection in heaven of each and every one of them will be with, and no faster than those they ruled over on earth.*

Promises, Promises - Chapter XXXI

Not only our deeds will follow us on our journey beyond mortality, but our intentions and the things we could have done but didn't do will also bind us after we leave the physical body:

> *Which is, that you will be bound in heaven until you accomplish what you might have done, but failed to do.*
>
> *And this is the penalty for neglecting, on earth, to fulfill the light that was given to you: You will, in heaven, accomplish without money, what you could have done with money.*
>
> *And the difference it requires to do a thing without means, as compared to what might be done by one with means, is the extra bondage and duration that will be upon your head and soul.*

Many of us struggle to understand our obligations. What is it that life requires of us? What are we responsible to do with our lives? Does it matter? How could such a remarkable gift as life not matter? What if everything matters to some degree or another? That might sound complicated, but if we do the best with what we have then we have fulfilled our responsibility:

> *The commandment of Creator is upon you, to do what you can, according to your highest light and ability to accomplish.*
>
> *In this respect, then, you will find no excuse, because you knew not the best way.*
>
> *Neither does it matter, the amount of your riches being less than another Man's riches. Nor will you find an excuse, in saying: I did more according to my means than did my neighbor.*
>
> *One Man will not be judged by another; but all will be judged according to the light of Creator in them and according to what He has given to them.*

The Earthbound Heavens and Fetals - Chapter XXXII

God said: Now, behold, O Man, I have declared my first and second resurrections to you. And in like manner is the third resurrection, but still higher. And so on are all the heavens of Creator, higher and higher, until the inhabitants of the heavens become very Lords and Gods.

Nevertheless, hear you, O Man, the wisdom of your God, and be appreciative of the way of resurrection being opened up to you.

Humanity has made incredible leaps in consciousness over the last two hundred years. One of the most important leaps in humanity's awareness is gaining the understanding that the human race is one family, and that we must learn to work together or perish. People have been dedicated to their immediate and extended families for thousands of years, wanting the best for their children and their children's children and so on. Now we are being faced with our responsibility to the human family and its wellbeing. The great question is how do we live together in peace and happiness?

Humanity's selfish behavior has created spiritual hells around the earth. Our ancestors, the angels of heaven, are calling us to cease the unnecessary and untimely destruction of our world family through lack of understanding and compassion, and the practice of war. And God is demanding that we cease our own destruction or suffer the consequences.

God speaks about the spiritual realms that are lower than the first resurrection and filled with incapacitated angels and drujas:

Now, I declare to you, there are angels lower than the first resurrection; being incapacitated, from various causes, from knowing who they are, whence they came, or whither they are going.

Yet, many of them know not words of speech, or signs, or tokens; but are as destitute of knowledge as young babes.

Many of them died in infancy; some of them were killed by abortion; some of them were idiots, and some of them deranged.

These beings or angels are bound to the earth and the peoples of the earth. They are not capable of growing on their own, any more than a young baby can. Because these lower angels are helpless, they cling to mortals to obtain life force and learn from them. These types of angels are called *fetals*. A fetal usually stays attached to a mortal for the mortal's entire life. Fetals learn about life from the examples of the mortals they are attached to:

Many of these live by fetal. Now, hear you, O Man, the judgment of your God: Half the people born into the world, including stillbirths and abortions, die in infancy. Therefore, there are a billion angel infants fetaled on the earth every thirty years.

These angels never obtain objective knowledge of the corporeal earth, but are compelled to learn subjectively earthly things through mortals upon whom they are fetaled. Judgment is rendered against all nations and peoples on the earth for this great darkness, these early deaths.

This text was written in 1882. Since then the infant mortality rate has declined dramatically. The number of abortions is not registered as infant mortality.

Gods Judgment against War

God speaks out against war and all who aid or abet war:

Now, aside from such angels, there are such as are slain in war, whose minds are in chaos, who, dying in the heat of passion and fear and anger, become wild and bound on battle-fields, or sometimes they stroll away into deserted houses and castles, and are lost, bewildered and unapproachable.

Of these, there are hundreds of millions; and they are in all countries and among all peoples in the world. They are distracted and tormented with their own fears and bewilderment.

> *Judgment is rendered against every nation and all people*
> *in the world, who carry on war, or who are accessory*
> *to war, by which any Man, created alive by Creator, is*
> *slain, in defense of any king or other ruler, or in defense*
> *of any country or government in all the world.*

Torture and other means of destruction create distorted spirits who practice evil against other spirits and mortals. These angels have been so damaged that they are no longer evolving, but are in declension:

And yet, aside from angels who are in chaos, there are hundreds of millions who are in declension, instead of resurrection.

Such angels are those who in mortal life were whipped and tortured in prisons, or were hanged, or otherwise put to death.

These angels take delight in evil instead of good. Sometimes they go about singly, and sometimes in gangs of hundreds and even thousands.

Judgment is rendered against all nations and peoples who use prisons as places for whipping and torturing prisoners; and against all nations and peoples who put to death by hanging, shooting, or in any way whatsoever, any prisoner or any person whom Creator created alive.

As our actions follow us into the next world, so we are bound by our actions. Those who promote or support war are bound in the first heaven until there is no more war on earth. Their work is to uplift humanity beyond war:

> *And this is the bondage I put upon all people who do not obey my judgments (against war) and conform to them:*

> *They will not rise above the first resurrection in heaven, while war remains upon the earth. Even though their bondage is a hundred years, or a thousand years, yet my judgment against them will not be put aside.*

Many people within the governments of the countries that engage in war don't want war. Still they support war by their participation in branches of the government that support war. During this time on earth, the pleas and prayers of well-intentioned people will not be answered if they are aiding or abetting war, and the angels will pull away from these governments:

> *Neither will I more consider the prayers of any king, or queen, or any other ruler, or any nation or people in all the world who engage in war, offensive or defensive, or who aid or abet war in any way whatsoever.*

When the higher angels withdraw their protection from a city or a government, chaos follows as the dark angels gain control:

> *And they will be afflicted with assassinations, and intriguers and despoilers, and with anarchy and riots and destruction.*

The edict: "Thou shalt not kill" was given to help us understand the sacredness of life and the need to protect life. When we lose this understanding, we create suffering for ourselves, for those who are killed, and the generations to come, which must live in the bondage of our ignorance:

For they will be made to understand that whoever Creator created
alive is sacred upon the earth; and that whoever heeds not these, my
judgments, sins against the Almighty.

Prejudice - Chapter XXXIII

The earth was purposefully designed with separate continents, islands, and races, so the different cultures could grow without interference. Now that we have grown into one world and one family, the Creator requires that we put away our prejudice and exclusivity, and embrace all peoples as our brothers and sisters:

Creator has said: In Kosmon I come, saying: Be you brethren upon the
face of the earth and upon the waters of the earth; these are the legacies
I bequeath to My children.

Jehovih has said: Be you a help and a profit to one another, judging
wisely of the differences which circumstances and places of habitation
have developed in the races of Man.

Now, I, your God, O Man, declare this judgment to you: Inasmuch as
your wisdom has surmounted the corporeal barrier, the ocean, between
you and your brother, it is meet and proper, that your soul surmount
the barrier of prejudice against your brother.

And that, instead of making laws against him, you will do the
opposite of this, and throw open the place of your habitation, and
your soul, and your love, to receive your brother, godlike, and with
open arms.

America has been a guiding light for the unfolding of the evolution of mankind by opening its gates and welcoming everyone. Yes, this country has made many wars and done greedy and selfish things, and now turns people away, but there is still time to turn in a more positive direction. America was destined to become a guiding light, and hopefully it will rise to fulfill the rest of its great destiny.

God encourages us in our progress toward becoming a one-world family. The heavens around the earth have become universal and no longer isolated by the countries that the mortals lived in on earth:

> *Behold, I have made the heavens of the earth universal;*
> *and established heavenly roadways around about the earth,*
> *that the angels of the different nations and peoples may be*
> *as angels of universal heavens, to help one another.*

Taxation

Not only are we to keep our countries open to all people to come and go freely, we are also to stop unequal taxation between countries:

> *Now, I declare to you, I will no longer have exclusiveness in any of the nations and peoples in all the world.*
>
> *Neither will there be taxes and duties of one nation or people against another. I will have all the ports open and free, and there will not be partisan taxation in favor of one nation against another, or of one people against another people.*
>
> *It is not excusable for you to say: Lo, the poor foreigner will come and consume my riches! You will say the opposite: Welcome, my poor brothers and sisters! Whatever is mine is yours also. Come and dwell within my country; it is ample, and Jehovih will provide for us.*

This may seem unachievable and unrealistic, but many things have come to pass that seemed impossible. If we want heaven on earth, we will have to create it.

True Government - Chapter XXXIV

God speaks about our governments and how they have fallen away from the original intention of working with the people and for the good of the people:

Your government has become a separate self from the people;
and the people are as servants, supporting the lawmakers, who
trade in projects and schemes for their own profit and glory.

Since the earliest days, all the governments of Man have drifted into
this. When a government no longer fills the grade, according to the
advancement of the people, behold, your God withdraws his heavenly
protection from that government.

And, straightway, the people run into anarchy. Lay not the blame of
anarchy and revolution and assassinations on the people; my judgment
is against the government in all cases.

These conditions of vengeance are but the fruit resulting from the
government's divergence from the will of Creator, and the march of
His light.

The concept of cause and effect is a basic law of our existence. If we choose selfishness and domination, we will reap the harvest, and so it is with governments. When the higher angels pull away from a government, the lower angels run wild and destroy the government:

Judgment is rendered against government where it does not
provide liberty to the people, and neglects providing means
for the development of the talents created with all.

In these respects, O Man, governments are measured and graded by
your God. And, whenever a government sets up itself to enforce and
strengthen itself by violence against justice to the multitude, behold, I
turn away from that government; and I call away my Lords and holy

angels. And, thereupon, drujas come upon that people, and the people fall upon their government, and destroy it.

Many of us have been asking "Thy kingdom come, thy will be done, on earth as it is in heaven." God gives a formula for determining the fall of any government or ruling body that is not moving toward manifesting heaven on earth:

The nearer the twain are to being one, that is, the government and the people, the nearer they are like to my heavenly kingdoms.

The more diverse the government is from the people, the farther it is from the kingdom of your God.

Let this be a guide to you, O Man, in prophesying the change and the overthrow of governments: According to the square of the distance a government is from Creator (which is Righteousness) so is the quickness of its coming change or destruction.

There is much debate about one-world government. There is distrust and caution regarding this concept, but there is also great potential for good. Whatever our personal preference, the Creator has His own agenda:

He is All One. For a people and their government to attain to be all one with each other, this is great strength, with a long existence and internal peace.

This, also, will you consider, O Man: All governments are tending toward oneness with one another. This is the march of Jehovih. None can stay Him. Governments that practice affiliation, to bring about reciprocal brotherhoods between governments, are on the right road toward the Father's everlasting kingdoms.

The Future of Governance - Chapter XXXV

The evolution of government continues on its own path toward dissolution. There is to come a time when governments are no longer necessary and the people will be able to rule themselves:

God said: Whoever lives with Jehovih is free from Jehovih. These need no Man's government; for they practice righteousness, peace, love, industry and wisdom, with due regard to one another.

Such is the Father's kingdom on earth. In which there will be no laws made by Man; neither will there be leaders or rulers. The progress of Man is toward this; the progress of the governments of Man should shape toward such a consummation.

New freedoms and liberty for all people will come with the coming of the Light in the Age of Kosmon:

Judgment is rendered against the laws and governments of Man in all cases where they prevent the liberty and choice of Man to his avocation and knowledge.

It is not sufficient for you to say: Behold, the public will be taken advantage of by ignorant pretenders. You have no right to say what the public will suffer, and thus base a law on prospective damage.

When the public have suffered, and when they, themselves, demand protection by such laws, then will such laws be made. To make such laws beforehand, is to sin against Creator.

God makes it very clear that we must strive to work together:

A government that sets up itself for itself, and against other governments, is a selfish government.

And your God rates it the same as a selfish Man, being diverse from Creator and his kingdoms.

Judgment is rendered against such a government. Neither my Lords nor my holy angels will bless that government.

The Age of Kosmon - Chapter XXXVI

God explains how he has prepared the earth for the Age of Kosmon. In order to build something new to replace something that is worn out, the old form must be removed and a new form built. The people necessary to build the new form must be trained in the skills necessary to accomplish the task, and there needs to be a blueprint of the new form:

God said: Behold the work of my hand, O Man: As you find an old house, no longer habitable, you send workmen to pull it down, and then, you send laborers to clear away the rubbish. And, afterward, you bring builders, and they lay a new foundation, larger and broader than the old one, and there they build you a new edifice, adapted with new improvements to the increase and requirements of your family.

Even so, your God has labored, for hundreds of years, to prepare to the generations of this day.

For I saw, beforehand, that Man would circumscribe the earth, and that all the nations and peoples there would become known to one another.

When the old form is a concept, a religion, or an organization, the same sequence is required, only we must also take into account the old forms contained within the minds of the people. In order to inspire people to let go of concepts that no longer apply to their lives in a productive manner, the people will need to understand that the previous concepts no longer serve them:

> *And now, behold, O Man, the wisdom of Creator previously: He had permitted corruptions and contradictions to creep into the sacred books of all of the said great religions, purposely and with design, so as to make easy the work of your God.*
>
> *And when I saw that the coming together of nations and peoples would require a new religious edifice, I perceived, also, that the old ones must be cleared away. And, behold, I, your God, went to work systematically, inspiring Man to accomplish even what Man has accomplished.*

For the upliftment of the minds of mankind, God had to prepare people that could do the work of removing the old edifice in preparation for the new:

> *I raised up scholars and infidels against these religions; inspiring them to attack the corruptions and contradictions in the sacred books of all these peoples.*

Sometimes it is not a good idea to put a new building exactly where the old structure was, especially if the people who have used the old structure are going to use the new one in the same manner without embracing the new possibilities that would allow them to progress in their consciousness. So, then, the new structure needs to be placed where there will not be prejudice and control regarding the use of the new structure:

> *And I made the beginning of the work of these infidels and scholars to correspond with the discovery of Guatama (America) by Columbus, and I kept them at their work for three hundred years, which was up to the time of the establishment of the republic of America, which I, your God, provided to be untrammeled by an established religion.*

The new structure was to be bigger and have much greater capacity to help mankind in its evolution:

> *For a hundred years, these, my laborers, have been at their work, stripping off and clearing away the prejudice of nations and peoples against one another.*
>
> *And then, behold, I came with my builders, and I prepared a new foundation, broader and wider and firmer, for an edifice adapted to all the nations and peoples in the world.*

There had to be people inspired to educate others to embrace their greater potential and abilities so the new edifice could be used to its fullest capacity. The people of the earth needed to become aware of their divine heritage:

> *First, I sent my miracle-workers forth into every quarter, saying to them: Whatsoever was done by the ancient Gods and Saviors, do you even so, and greater.*
>
> *For I will show to all the world that no Man nor God is worthy to be worshipped because of miracles.*
>
> *My testimony and my witnesses are hundreds of thousands. I do not hide the work of my hand and of my angels in a corner; I extend them abroad over the earth; I manifest in the cities and country places;*
>
> *I prove to all peoples, that common men and women can do the miracles for which Gods and Saviors have been worshipped.*

Once the people began to realize their own potential, they had to be taught that working together with others for a common good was essential for the good of all, and for their own happiness:

> *And I have shown also, that only by harmony and the union of many, can any great good come to the generations of men.*

The Coming of the Kosmon Age - Chapter XXXVII

God explains how the spiritual worlds work with humanity to bring about the upliftment of the world:

> God said: Do not think, O Man, that your God goes about a work without a system and order.
>
> Verily these are the first of my considerations. First, I send my loo'is, my masters of generations, down to the earth, to the nations and peoples where I design to build my edifice.
>
> And my loo'is, by inspiration, controls the marriages of certain mortals that heirs may be born into the world suited to the work I have on hand.

When people are born for a particular work in the world by the assistance of the loo'is, they are then partnered and inspired by other angels to fulfill their destiny:

> For many generations, my loo'is labor to this end, raising up thousands and tens of thousands of mortal heirs according to my commandments. So, O Man, since four hundred years my loo' is shaped mortal births to bring about the armies of your God.

God has a plan to assist in the upliftment of humanity, but he needs the cooperation of aware people on earth to work for the upliftment of humanity:

> Thus, O Man, your God knew beforehand what part and what place each and every one of his mortal laborers was adapted to.
>
> And through my Lords and generals and captains of my angel hosts, I commanded Man to fall to work on my building.

Some to heal the sick, some to work signs and miracles, some to lecture, some to write, and so on, every one according to the work of his adaptation.

The great changes and upheavals of our time have indeed been (and are) the birthing of a new world, a world that has been destined for this time since the beginning of Man:

And all of this is to one purpose; not to build up or exalt any Man, nor God, nor religion, but to found Creator's kingdom on earth. To give Man the system of universal peace, love, harmony and Kosmon, adapted to all nations and peoples in all the world.

God gave the angels orders to support people who used their God-given gifts to help others:

And to whoever does a good work in truth, righteousness, wisdom and love, my holy angels are commanded to extend their sphere of usefulness and light.

And to those who were unable to use their gifts unselfishly, the angels withdrew their support, and many people fell under the influence of lesser forces:

And I commanded my holy angels to withdraw from all mortals who were not working for Creator's new kingdom, who were of no profit in the resurrection of Man; and, behold, this was also done.

And it came to pass, that many whom I had designed for exalted work, fell into the hands of drujas. And they held conferences, and were divided, man against man, and woman against woman; full of boasting and shortsighted wisdom, seeking the applause of the multitude.

In choosing, we are chosen:

> *And, so, my angels sifted them and sorted them, in order to find such*
> *as were willing to sacrifice self for the sake of the Father's kingdom.*
> *These I drew aside, and I said to them:*

> *You, that choose to serve Creator, behold,*
> *Creator has chosen you also.*

The Heirs of Kosmon - Chapters XXXVIII

When the new edifice comes into being, who will inhabit it and who will manifest its purpose?

> *God said: I say to you, O Man, pursue your wisdom after the manner*
> *of your God.*

> *I go to the beginning; I do not labor as much to convert adults, as I*
> *labor to prepare the minds of the young.*

> *I say to you: The new edifice will be of all that was good of the past, of*
> *things proven in heaven and on earth. Also, I say to you, it will be of*
> *the young, and not of the adult.*

Those who were prepared to build the new edifice may not be those who will inherit the new world. They are the preparers of the way and they will be inspired to gather the orphans and castaways of our society and take them into communities away from the old forms of society, in order for them to learn of the new world:

> *They will gather up orphans and castaways in infancy, and take them*
> *into colonies, hundreds and thousands of them.*

> *Behold, it has been proven in the warrior and pugilist how to raise*
> *a savage man, by flesh diet and inharmonious surroundings; and in*

nations and tribes of peace, how to raise a virtuous and industrious man, on herbs and fruit diet.

And yet, above all things, you will preserve liberty to all, with pleasant and enjoyable discipline for everything, after the manner of my heavenly kingdoms.

And you will remember this, so that every faculty in every one will be cultivated to the utmost.

You will teach them from the beginning that the eye of Creator is upon them, and that His hand is stretched over them, to bless them, according to their goodness, purity, love, gentleness and wisdom.

And that they will not own nor possess individually; but that all things are Creators, and they, themselves, are angels in mortal form, created by Creator to rejoice and to help one another forever.

The New World - Chapter XXXIX

God describes briefly what the new communities will be like, and the capacities that can be obtained by living a new way of life outside of the old edifice:

And these things will come to pass with these people: They will abjure war; they will be non-resistant; they will have su'is, and will see without their mortal eyes, and hear without their mortal ears. My angels will appear before them, and walk with them, talking to them, and teaching them of my kingdoms.

And mortals will recover, from the libraries in heaven, things that have been lost on the earth as to languages and histories of tens of thousands of years ago.

And mortals will prophesy truly of things in heaven and on the earth. And many will attain adeptism, and, in spirit, go out of their mortal bodies, and appear hundreds of miles away and there make themselves known; and they will return again to their mortal bodies, unharmed.

All these, and even greater things, will my angels teach them.

Do not flatter yourself, O Man, that these things can come in Uz, or that they can come suddenly. They can neither come to Uzians, nor can they come suddenly.

It is not the work of your God in this cycle to raise up any one to become worshipful because of such wonders; it is my work to show Man how he will attain to these things himself.

I do not come, in this day, to call sinners to repentance, nor to gather up the lost sheep of Israel. I come now to the wise and pure, which have fulfilled the former commandments. I come to give them a new lesson, which is, to show them how to build the Father's kingdom on earth.

I come to raise up a new people in the world, greater than has ever been. Those that I sent have cleared away the old edifice. I do not come as a destroyer I come as a builder.

God has handed off to us the knowledge of how to live on earth and we are responsible to make it a reality:

Into your hands, O Man, I give the key to the heavenly kingdoms.

Remember, the password which admits you to the all highest kingdoms is JEHOVIH, THE I AM.

NOTES:

The Book of Inspiration

You are of inspiration made, said Jehovih. I made you a corporeal body, and I wrote upon it. You are the result. And I made you susceptible, so all things external to yourself could write upon you. The sum of these is your knowledge. As it is with you, so is it with all Man, and with all the living which I created. Nor is there any knowledge in the world, but what I gave. All of it is My inspiration.

The Creator Speaks - Chapter I

The Book of Inspiration is written from the perspective of the Creator. It explains more about Him and our relationship to Him. Tae represents the Creator speaking through humanity in writings and other forms of inspiration:

> *These are the words of Tae, in Kosmon: I am Light; I am Central, but Boundless, said Jehovih.*

We are born into a physical body to localize our spirit. This is how we learn about the physical and spiritual realities, because it gives us a frame of reference through relationship with matter that allows us to understand ourselves. Being in a physical body allows us to learn how to focus our consciousness and learn the basics of cause and effect. It allows us to discover who we are and why we exist:

> *Your corpor I made, in which to localize you; to mature your entity. Without Me, you would not have come to life. You are as the end of a ray of light from My Person. And you are focalized in your corporeal body.*

One of the greater questions of existence is, "Where did I come from and what was I before I was born?" The Book of Inspiration says we did not exist before we were brought to life in physical form. By an impulse of Light from the Creator, our form and our soul were brought to life together. We are a ray of Light from the Creator. At the moment of conception, a divine spark of Light ignites the cells and life begins:

> *You were nothing; though all things that constitute you were before. These I drove together, and quickened. Thus I made you.*

At that magical moment of conception, out of nothing (or everything) we arrive in mortal form. The body grows itself. The cells know what to do. They multiply and the hair begins to grow, the teeth come in, and the mind begins to understand and formulate thoughts. Who and what we are is the Creator, and the Creator is Light. All life requires Light to exist and the Creator is that Light:

> *As out of corpor I made your corporeal body, so, out of My Light, which is My Very Self, I built you up in spirit, with consciousness that you are.*

As we grow in understanding, we take on more and more Light. Do we have free will? Yes and no. We have our own thoughts, but do we? Do you wonder if you have ever had a truly original thought? Have you ever questioned where your thoughts come from, or why you think a certain way? Are you in full control of who you are and what you do? The Book of Inspiration challenges us in this regard:

> *Out of Myself grows your spirit.*

We are Light, physically and spiritually. We can't separate the physical from the spiritual in mortal life, and yet they separate when we die. Our spirit doesn't arrive here fully grown; it grows by the presence of the All Light. We arrive as an individual spark of Light and begin our eternal becoming. So, where does our knowledge come from? How does our awareness grow?

> *Neither can you, of your own self, manufacture or acquire or take to yourself, one new thought, or idea, or invention.*

This statement is pretty hard on the ego, but it is easy to understand if we give some time to this possibility. Watch a child grow and you will see how it is in a constant state of learning from everything around it:

> *All thought and knowledge and judgment which you have, I gave to you.*

How can the Creator possibly give everyone on the planet his or her thoughts every moment? This statement forces us to expand our consciousness and embrace a vast concept: We exist inside the Creator, which is everything there is, seen and unseen. We take a breath, and we are breathing in the Divine. We hear a bird singing, and we are hearing the Creator singing. Our heartbeat is the presence of the Divine. We do not keep our heart beating or consciously manage our every breath and thought. Life flows through us. Life sings through us. The Creator lives around and through us in every moment:

All your corporeal part is, therefore, of Me and through Me. Even so is your spirit of Me also.

The physical body has been referred to as the temple of God. It is Eoih's gift to us to house our individual spirit and the soul spark of the Creator. If we could remember this every day, we would take better care of each other and ourselves.

By My Inspiration - Chapter II

Man was made to receive knowledge from his surroundings. As we grow older, we tend to think that the childhood phase of our learning is over and we live as adults. We create ideas, design structures, and build organizations. We believe we are independent entities with our own ideas and abilities. Yes, we are individuals, and yet our knowledge is not our own. It is but a gleaning of the presence of the Divine:

I made you a corporeal body, and I wrote upon it. You are the result. And I made you susceptible, so all things external to yourself could write upon you. The sum of these is your knowledge.

The more aware we become of our surroundings, our thoughts, others thoughts, and the workings of this infinite universe, the more we take in the Light of creation, the Creator:

The sum of all of Man's knowledge is but Man's capacity to perceive My Light.

We tend to judge our self-worth by how much we have learned and how much we can do. As a productive member of our society this would be true. As a creation of the All Light we are gathers of the Light of the Creator and co-creators of our own being. Our value is priceless and our task is eternal. When we live in this understanding, we live in humility and gratitude:

> *A man holds a magnifying lens to the sun, and he lights a fire, but yet the lens did not contain the heat. After such manner have you accumulated knowledge; yet, no knowledge was of your own begetting, but all came from Me. I gave it all.*

Look at all the incredible things humans have created in the past hundred years. The evolutionary leaps that we have made are amazing. We pride ourselves with how fast we are progressing in our understanding of how life works. The Hubble telescope shows us the galaxies and more. The microscope shows us the minute particles of matter. We are becoming a great civilization:

> *The increase in knowledge now upon the earth, with all the races of men, is only the increase I gave. Man, himself, created none of it. Neither can you create one thought, nor idea, nor impulse.*
>
> *You can only gather together from My harvests, or from Me in Person.*

I Made You - Chapter III

Why are we made the way we are? Why do we need to experience life on earth?

> *The eye of Man I made to obtain knowledge by light; but the ear of Man I made to obtain knowledge from darkness, and within darkness, said Jehovih.*

The power of touch I gave to Man, by which he might learn of things their adaptability and compatibility and incompatibility with himself.

These are the corporeal doorways I gave to you, O Man, where you might receive knowledge from Me and My creations, consciously to yourself.

Our lives are filled with inspiration in every moment. We are constantly impressed with feelings and thoughts. We are building ourselves every moment through the impressions, experiences and inspirations we receive and how we interrupt them:

Whatever is charged upon these doorways of My soul is inspiration. When you see bread, you are inspired to eat; when you see a horse, you are inspired to ride; when you touch a nettle, you are inspired with pain.

Yet, in all cases, you must have practice before you can comprehend the inspiration that comes to you from these external things.

As we grow and learn we are storing information. Much like a computer we are accumulating knowledge:

Jehovih said: I made you as a storehouse, and as a book that was written before. And I gave to you power to re-read your stores and your book, within your soul.

As we seek to know the Creator, we will be able to see His workings, His presence in all things, including in each other and ourselves:

My impression upon you is inspiration, but you must realize My inspiration in order to know Me.

Most of the time, life impresses itself upon us, and we just follow our every impulse. We think, "I'm hungry. Why am I hungry? I'm hungry because I need to eat." Sometimes this is true. Sometimes we see an advertisement about food that looks really good, and we get hungry. We walk by an ice cream store and we want ice cream. There is nothing wrong with being influenced by our surroundings. But if we want to understand who we are and our relationship with the Creator, we need to become more aware of where our inspirations come from.

Imagine talking with someone who is upset about politics and you get upset, too. Imagine someone who is really down and depressed visits you, and by the time the person leaves, you are also depressed. Something or someone is always influencing us. If we can become aware enough to see where and why we are influenced, then we will gain a clearer understanding of ourselves, the sources of our inspiration, and what our appropriate responses should be:

> *So, also, I come to you and give you inspiration, but you do not discern Me. Another man discerns My Presence, and My inspiration. He hears Me speak; he sees My Person. Yet, I am with both alike.*

> *One man is sensitive, as a plate for a picture, and he catches My Light instantly, and knows it is from Me. Another one says: A sudden thought struck me! But he does not discern where it came from.*

By My Light - Chapter IV

Light gives us the ability to see, hear, and learn. Our learning comes in two forms, the physical (corporeal) senses and the spiritual senses:

> *When the infant is young, My Light is its first knowledge, said the Creator. It sees Me and hears Me; and it sees and hears My angels.*

> *By the pressure of My Light upon its corporeal eyes and ears, it learns to see and hear corporeally.*

> *This is the beginning of two senses, which I created to grow parallel to each other and equal in strength. But the infant, being in the corporeal world, heeds more the things that appeal to the corporeal senses than such as appeal to the spiritual senses.*

Depending on which of our two senses is the strongest, the physical or the spiritual, a person will relate to life as either a skeptic or a believer:

> *So that one person grows up, forgetting Me and My angels. He is a skeptic. But another person grows up, remembering Me and My angels. He is a believer.*

Again, we are asked to consider the Creator as being so vast that nothing more exists. The Creator is the essence of all things. By Eoih's presence all things live and move. The Creator permeates all things, all people, all universes, and all thought:

> *By My Presence and inspiration upon you, I taught you I am the I AM, a Person.*
> *By the inspiration and presence of My angels, I taught you of them also.*
> *My inspiration upon the bird causes it to sing.*
> *By My Presence I teach it to build its nest.*
> *By My Presence I color one rose red, and another white.*
> *Proof of My Person is in the harmony of the whole, and of every one being a person of itself, perfect in its order.*

The Voice - Chapter V

The Creator explains the two kinds of voices that inspire us. One is audible and the other is silent. We are inspired by the Creator according to the degree of our purity and the health of our body, our mind and our spirit:

> *In proportion as Man is clear in his corporeality and in his spirit, so he discerns My inspiration. Two kinds of voices I have, said the Creator: The silent voice and the audible voice.*
>
> *I created all of Man susceptible to one or the other of My voices, and many to both.*

The audible voice of the Creator can be heard in the sounds of nature, in music, and in conversation with others. When the birds and crickets and frogs sing, we hear the song of Divine Presence. The storms and the rain and the wind in the trees, they are all the voice of Eoih. A symphony or someone talking is the expression of the Creator. Nature Herself is the Creator speaking to us, as is our neighbor. In the quiet moments, in the stillness, and when we take the time to listen deeply, we can hear the voice of the Creator through our inspirations and our dreams:

> *One person hears My voice in the breeze, and in thunder, and in music. One person hears My voice in the flowers of the field, and in the scenery of the mountains. And yet another feels My inspiration; and he skips up the mountainside, and does not tire on the way. He that neither sees nor feels My inspiration, goes up the mountain in great labor.*

We receive that which we focus on. When we are in balance in our relationship to the physical world and the spiritual world, we can receive the inspirations we need from both of them:

> *Perfect Manhood I created possible, in equal corporeal and spiritual senses. Strong corporeal senses and weak spiritual senses detract Man from My Presence, and make him infidel (an unbeliever) to My Person. Such a man denies My inspiration and the inspiration of My angels.*

By My Presence - Chapter VI

By the presence of Jehovih all living things of this earth manifest a unique piece of the Creator. He is the Light that moves through all things and gives life to all things:

> *I am One Spirit, said Jehovih. My quickening power is upon all the living; because of this, they live and move.*

According to the different structure of the living, so is My inspiration manifested by them. One, as the hare, runs away in cowardice; another, as a lion, is ferocious; another, without judgment, as the serpent.

And as to Man: One is inspired to music; another to mathematics; another to seership, and so on.

To all of these I am the One, the Universal Inspirer that moves all of them.

The First Creation

During the first part of earth's creation, the earth was encircled with poisonous gases. The Creator drove these gases into the vegetable kingdom and then into the serpents of the world, thus clearing the atmosphere in preparation for the animal kingdom:

When the earth was encircled with poisonous gases, I created poisonous vines and weeds and trees and all kinds of herbs, rich-growing upon the earth.

Thus, from destroying gases and from earth-substance I created the vegetable world. And, in that day, all growing things upon the earth, which I had created, were poison to animal life.

And the serpents I created were carnivorous, feeding upon one another. I created them self-impregnating.

Thus I drove the poison of the air down into vegetation, and from there into the animal world; In this way I purified the air of heaven.

Then the Creator covered up the vegetation with falling nebulae to provide oil and tar for Man's future use. Again, the vortex was changed, and nebulae rained down upon the earth:

Then I overcast the earth with falling nebulae, and covered up the poisons growing upon the earth, and they were turned to oil and coal.

When the Father drives forth His worlds in the heavens, they gather a sufficiency of all things. So it happens that when a corporeal world is yet new and young it is carried forth, not by random, but purposely, in the regions suited to it.

Hence there is a time of se mu, a time for falling nebulae, to bury deep the forests and se'muan beds, to provide coal and manure for a time thereafter.

So is there a time when the earth passes a region in the firmament when sand and oil are rained upon it and covered up, and gases bound and sealed up for the coming generations of Man.

The Second Creation

The second creation appeared on the earth and the animal kingdom came into being and Man was created:

Then, I made a new creation; giving feet and legs and bones to the animals I designed for the earth.

And when the earth was ripe for Man, then I created them; male and female, I created those of the second creation.

The Creator took from all substances of the first and second creation to create Man. We are made from the elements of all living things that came before us. We are intimately connected to creation because we are all of creation, and our relationship with creation is essential in order for us to know who we are:

Nevertheless, I had given to Man, and thus made him, out of the dissolved elements of every living thing that had preceded him.

It is as if all of creation came together in the form of Man in order to have a fuller expression of itself:

> *And Man partook of the first and the second creations. After the manner of every animal on the earth, so I created Man; with all the characteristics of all of them, so I created him, male and female I created them.*

Because Man was still part of the animal kingdom, he was unconscious of himself, so the Creator called upon angels from other worlds to come to the earth and to teach Man who he was and to raise him up above the animal kingdoms:

> *And Man was unconscious of his creation, not knowing from where he came; or which was his own species. And I sent angels to Man, to teach him who he was, and to rouse him up to his capabilities, for which I created him.*
>
> *And my angels drew from Man's side, substance, and in this way took on corporeal forms, and the angels dwelt with Man as helpmates to make Man understand.*

The angels took etheric substance from Man's side (the rib) to manifest in the physical world and they partook of the Tree of Life and cohabited with the tribes of the original man and a new race was born called Man.

Man's Capacity - Chapter VII

We have become accustomed to thinking of animals as dumb because they do not speak our language. Animals speak in telepathic ways, and we can learn to hear them. Perhaps in the early creation, Man could understand the audible or telepathic speech of the animals:

> *And when My angels had taught Man speech, making Man name all the animals in the world, after the names the animals called themselves, I commanded My angels to come away from Man, for a season.*

When Man had reached a level of consciousness in which they could relate to the animal kingdom, and the Creator, the angels left their mortal form.

What is it that makes us different from the other creatures of this world?

> To My angels I said: Behold, of all the animals I created in the world, to Man only gave I the capacity to transmit knowledge to his brethren by words. And to Man only I gave capacity to comprehend an idea of Me, his Creator. Nevertheless I inspire all living animals which I created but they know it not.

The animal kingdom is naturally in concert with Creator:

> I inspire the spider to make its net; the bird to build her nest; the wild goose to fly to the south, before the winter comes; the mare to neigh for her colt; the ant to lay in its stores; the bees to dwell in a queendom; and so on, every living creature do I move and control by My inspiration upon them.
>
> Males and females, I inspire to come together at times and seasons, and then to live apart during gestation. These I keep before Man as a lesson of the wisdom of My inspiration.

Man is not the same as the animals. He has the ability to ask the deeper questions and know the Creator in ways that the rest of the kingdom cannot. The animal kingdom knows the Creator directly in ways that few mortals ever achieve:

> By direct inspiration do I move upon all the animals I created. This I also created possible to Man, separate from indirect inspiration.

Are we more intelligent than a dolphin, an elephant, or a dog? Are we more capacitated than the rest of creation?

I have also given Man capacity to attain to know My inspiration
in contradistinction from the inspiration he receives from his
surroundings. I gave this capacity to no other creature.

The question arises: How does one know when we are being inspired directly by the Creator or by our surroundings?

What comes of Me is without pain or injury to anyone, and with liberty
to all. Such are My inspirations. What moves Man in consonance and
wisdom, and to life is My inspiration. What moves Man in dissonance
and folly, and to death is inspiration from Man's surroundings.

Direct and Indirect Inspiration - Chapter VIII

If the Creator is everything and everywhere, then how can the Creator not inspire us? We are inspired by the Ever-Present, either directly or indirectly. We could say that everything that is alive is the primary creation and, thus, is the body of the Creator. This would be trees and stars and bugs and bears and mountains and humans. These are things that are alive in a way that is more than just molecular movement. The Primary Creation is a direct experience of the Creator.

Although all inspiration goes from Me to all the living, directly, yet I also
created Man susceptible to indirect inspiration from all My creations.

The secondary creation is an expression of the primary creation. It is an indirect inspiration and it lacks the life essence of the primary creation. The secondary creation includes such things as cement, cars, buildings, art, music, and literature. These things are a reflection of the primary creation, but they do not live in the same sense as a tree, an animal, or a person does. The primary creation has the ability to inspire and uplift humanity to create expressions of the beauty of the primary creation. It carries life force that renews us and reminds us of our essence. The secondary is a reflection of the primary creation and can either inspire us or deter us from our connection to the Creator.

The quality of what we create will be in accordance with our alignment to the Creator:

> *Whatsoever receives from Me direct, is in harmony with Me*

The clearest inspiration we can have is directly from the Creator, and everyone is capable of direct inspiration. An individual's aptitude toward direct inspiration depends on the environment, the education of family and schools, and genetic inheritance:

> *But because I made Man capacitated to receive inspiration from all things, he manifests both evil and good; according to his birth and surroundings, so is Man good or bad.*

Original Sin

Are we inherently evil?

> *I did not create Man to destruction but to life, wisdom, peace and love toward all. When Man practices virtue, wisdom, truth and love to all, his inspiration is from Me directly. When Man practices destruction and selfishness his inspiration is indirectly from Me, through the conflict of his surroundings.*

We are not left alone on earth to figure this all out for ourselves. Our guardian angels are always present to inspire us:

> *And I sent my angels to Man, teaching him how to distinguish the difference in the inspirations upon him, that he might govern himself accordingly.*

Here is a list of direct inspirations and indirect inspirations:

And My angels said to Man: Become one with your Creator; these are His direct inspirations:

- *To love your Creator above all else, and your neighbor as yourself.*
- *To give delights only, and not pain.*
- *To not kill.*
- *To not do violently against His creatures.*
- *To be considerate of the liberty of all the living.*
- *To not interdict the happiness and hope of others, only where you can return a transcendent glory and hope in place of this.*

But these are your evil inspirations, O Man; these come from your birth and surroundings, formerly called Satan:

- *To kill.*
- *To slander.*
- *To punish.*
- *To destroy Jehovih's created beings.*
- *To strive for yourself, above another.*
- *To gratify your flesh at the expense of purity or wisdom.*
- *To be false to Jehovih.*
- *To be false to yourself.*
- *To speak falsely.*
- *To covet anothers.*
- *To cohabit in the gestative period.*
- *To engage in strife, or to aid and abet conflicts, which are the fruit of carnivorous food, transmitted in birth.*

Judging Ourselves - Chapter IX

What is our responsibility regarding discernment and judgment? As a child comes of age and is expected to judge for him or herself what is right and wrong, so it is with humanity. We are coming of age, and we are now expected to ask the deeper questions and judge for ourselves:

You will be your own judge in all things. Behold, I sent My God to judge you; but you will also judge the judgments of your God; and, afterward, you will judge yourself in the same way. As a perpetual judge I created you, not only to judge yourself and the entire world besides, but you will judge Me, your Creator.

Life on earth is preparation for life in the immortal realms of Light. As we grow, so must our degree of discernment increase. We should not be afraid to question the validity others opinions. This is not about confrontation and calling another down and I'm right and you are wrong. It is about seeking truth and not just accepting someone else's perspective based on their social standing. We must learn to rely on our own ability to relate to the Creator and to gain our own truth:

I have given you many sacred books, and I said to you: Save you judge them, you will be caught in a snare; I charge you, that you will accept nothing from men, or angels, or Gods.

But you will rely on your own inspiration from your Creator. Such is My word, which I speak to your own soul.

No secondhand knowledge, another's experience or version of reality, or a religion is binding. We are free to accept or reject information, and we are responsible to make our own decisions about what we accept. We can no longer have another authority make these decisions for us. We are now personally responsible for what we accept or reject:

What comes to you from a man is indirect inspiration; what comes from an angel is indirect and what comes from the Gods is indirect.

We are in the information age. Anything we want to know is at our fingertips. Google the earth and see everything. Every question has an answer, research papers, and scientific data. It is overwhelming and extraordinary. But all the information in the world cannot give us direct access to the Creator. Only by reaching for the deeper knowing within all life and ourselves can we access the Creator directly:

> *No direct inspiration of Me can come to you from a book, nor a sermon, nor from anything in all My creations but only from Me, your Creator.*

I AM With You - Chapter X

Our evolution has been an unfoldment of our innate abilities, an awakening of our true nature. We have come a long way since the beginning of Man and we are about to make another leap of consciousness into our greater destiny:

> *In the first creation none heard Me, or saw Me, said the Creator. And, even to this day, many men deny Me and My Person.*

It will take effort and a willingness to let go of things that hold us back:

> *To teach you, O Man, that you should be considerate of your brother's talents, behold, what a labor for My Gods and ministering angels!*

> - *To show you that no two people see anything alike that I created;*
> - *To make you cautious, that, because you cannot hear Me, you will not judge your brother who can hear Me;*
> - *To induce you thus and thus, without interfering with your liberty;*
> - *To make you watchful, to learn by your own inspiration from Me;*
> - *To make you skeptical to others versions of My words, and yet make you try to discover My words and My Person, of your own self, to see Me and hear Me.*

The next quote speaks of how difficult it was for mankind to hear the Creator directly in ages past. Now many can hear the voice of the Creator, and eventually everyone will hear it. What would life on earth be like if everyone could hear the Creator's voice?

Now, behold, in the olden times, only here and there, one, in all the world, could be made to comprehend Me. As you may say to the beast in the field, or to the dog, the most knowing of animals: Jehovih! Jehovih! and they will not hear you with understanding.

So it was with nearly all the world, in the olden times. Today, I have quickened many. Tomorrow, the whole of the people in all the world will know Me.

As science continues to uncover the workings of the universe, it is starting to merge with spiritual perspectives regarding the workings of the unseen forces of life. People everywhere can see the pictures of space and stars and galaxies. We can watch stars being born and stars dying. We can watch galaxies colliding. We have reached a point at which we are tracking the Creator's movements under the microscope and in the stars:

You have put Me away and said: Natural law! Moral law! Divine law! Instinct! Reflection! Intuition! Second sight! I say to you: I have abolished all these things. I will have them no more, forever!

The Creator demands that we reach for an even deeper understanding of who He is, telling us, "I am Life, look deeper. I am everywhere in everything." Life is the Creator expressing Himself through all form, all time, and all space, and that includes us:

I have no laws; I do by virtue of My own Presence.
I am not far away; behold, I am with you.
I gave no instinct to any creature under the sun.
By My Presence they do what they do.

If we could relinquish our belief in mankind's opinions as law and seek the source of All That Is, we would find the answers to all our questions:

I give no tuition by intuition;
I am the Cause to all, and for all.
I am the most easily understood of all things.

My Hand is ready to whoever will reach out to Me.

My Voice is ready and clear to whoever will turn away from other things, and away from philosophies and ambiguous words, serving Me in good works.

My Light is present and answers all who follow their all-highest knowledge.

I Am With All My Living - Chapter XI

We are moving into a time on earth when religions, as we have known them, will cease to exist, and all humanity will move into a new relationship with the Creator, and with each other. It is time for everyone to be free and hear the Creator in his or her own way:

> *Do not seek to spread My gospels, and entice followers to this, or that, said Jehovih. Neither go about preaching, saying: Thus said the Creator!*
> *Let all men hear Me in their own way.*
> *No man will follow another.*
> *I will have no sect.*
> *I will have no creed.*
>
> *I am not exclusive, but I am with all My living creatures.*

Fear is a major driving element that keeps us bound to the knowledge and opinion of others. We fall back on authority and public consensus to find truth. Now each of us is directed to find the Creator in our own way and in our own time. The soul of Man will blossom and humanity will awaken to whatever the truth is without oppression or consensus.

When we realize there is a Creator and act to the best of our ability, we will have the support we need to inspire and guide us on our journey into the Light. This is not so much about choosing sides, as it is about aligning to the essence of life within and around us. We are not separate. When we reach out to feel and understand life, we begin to activate a partnership that awaits our awakening.

Creator has said this to humanity many times in the past, but we have usually turned our trust toward someone we could see and touch. Now, the Creator is calling His children back home:

> To those who choose Me, practicing their all-highest light, I am a shield and fortification against all darkness, and against all evil and contention.

How does choosing the Creator provide a shield and protection against the darkness? By the laws of attraction we call to ourselves the energy of darkness or energy of the Light. By seeing and feeling the presence of the Divine all around us, we live in a state of being that is not ruled by fear, loneliness, or greed. We draw to us the Light that feeds our soul, our mind, and our heart with love, courage, and compassion. We learn to live in the Light and not in the darkness.

The Creator goes on to talk of true liberty, of learning to be free of the opinions of others, and finding the truth for ourselves directly from the Creator:

> I said to Man: Be free! Learn to know liberty! Think for yourself!
> Study your Creator in all things and in yourself in particular!
> Turn away from your elder brothers; come to the All Highest Fountain.
> Do not be confounded with abstruse reasoning; cut all things short,
> Godlike; learn of the Creator and His creations, there is nothing more.
>
> You are one of the seeds of Jehovih, and were planted by His Hand.
> Be you free from all the world.

The Influence of Diet - Chapter XII

The course of our evolution is different from other creatures on the earth for our destiny is very different from all the other creatures:

Man only, of all My created animals, I created imperfect in his order,
said the Creator. The most devoid of knowledge, and the most helpless
of animals, I created Man Thus differently I created Man from all
other things on earth; but I gave him the foundation whereon he might
attain to perfection in all the attributes of My other living creatures.

Diet and environment are major elements for evolving into our higher potential. The Creator talks about the influence of diet on one's ability to hear the Creator directly:

And I said to Man:
Be observant of what you will eat and drink and where you will dwell
by day and sleep by night.
For all things will write upon your soul the character
and the kind whereof they are made.

If you will be gentle, like a lamb, and non-resistant and docile, so you
may obtain great knowledge, feed upon herbs and fruits and cereals.
And your blood will be pure and cool, and charged with food for your
spirit, in peace and love.

But if you will be ferocious, like a carnivorous beast, then you will feed
upon flesh and fish, and your blood will be hot, and your spirit will be
stirred with passion and anger and contention and tattling and war
and jealousy and love of vengeance. For whatever you charge your blood
with, will be charged upon your spirit.

If one takes this statement seriously, then whatever we put in our mouth or our veins, could be thought of as strengthening or weakening our spirit. What about when we drink alcohol, take drugs, eat junk food, or eat too much or eat too little? How are we tending our body and our spirit?

Because you cannot feed on fish nor flesh but through destruction to
death, even so, destruction to death will come upon your soul.

How can the soul be destroyed? This quote means that the soul will be covered over and unable to express itself until death releases it from the body. It will be as if it were dead until it is released from the physical body by death.

The density of flesh and blood makes it very difficult for the soul to express itself:

From your own blood will your spirit be inspired
even according to what your blood contains.

When we live by the destruction of another living being, we destroy our soul's ability to be fully present in mortal life. According to the health and content of our blood, our spirit is strengthened or weakened. The subtle or spiritual part of all living things, plants and animals, is what nurtures our spirit. This is why it is so important to be aware of what we eat:

As through corpor your corporeal part is nurtured, so through the
gaseous, atmospherean part is your spirit nurtured.

As Man is both a physical and spiritual being, so are all living things on earth. In alchemical terms, every plant has a spiritual essence. In new science this is the quantum field. The subtle preparations of homeopathic formulations and flower essences focus on the spirit of the plant. The physical world is the impotent part and the spiritual world is the potent part of life. The most powerful part of a person is their spirit, and so it is with all that is alive. All food has a spiritual component. When we consume an orange or a fish, we are also feeding our spirit with the spirit of that food.

The Creator is specific with regard to the effects of eating flesh foods, be it fish, fowl, or four-legged creatures of the earth. Taking their life into our body creates conflict and contention, which can lead to disease, both physical and mental, and a propensity to engage in conflict of word or action. The pain and fear of the creatures we destroy impresses itself upon our body and spirit when we eat them.

We are being called to let go of living from the death of sentient beings and become a truly humane and peaceful race of people. We are not just called to do this; we are being required to change by life itself calling us to a new and greater level of life, awareness and responsibility:

> *It is the contamination of the blood of Man by carnivorous food, whereon you should ponder. Like to like I created all the living. Whoever makes themselves carnivorous, cannot escape conflict and contention within his own members, soul and body. Until the earth was circumscribed, I gave Man carnivorous food; today, I make it poison to him.*

This time on earth is to be the fruition of Man's evolution. We are being called to become aware of the quantum field within and around all life. Now is the time when we will indeed turn our guns into plowshares and create heaven on earth:

> *As there was a time when I created every animal perfect in its order; so also will such a time come to Man. And now is the dawn of that time. Hence, I named it Kosmon.*

I Gave You Liberty - Chapter XIII

The Creator talks about our responsibilities. Human beings have a habit of blaming other people and circumstances for their situations. Here is a clear statement about our personal responsibility:

> *The Creator said: Because I gave you liberty, you are responsible for all you are, and for all you make of yourself, and for all that will come to you, and for your peace and happiness, both in this world and the next.*

We are responsible for what we choose to eat and how we care for ourselves, each other, and all life forms on this world:

> *Because you made yourself carnivorous, the fault is your own. I placed before you the herbivorous animals and the carnivorous animals; and I gave you eyes to look upon them as to their behavior, whether ferocious and destructive, or peaceful, patient and docile.*
>
> *And I spoke to your soul, saying: Look, judge for yourself as to what you will eat; behold the order of My creations and the result upon all My living creatures.*
>
> *Hence, you are accountable to yourself, and responsible to all the world for having made your corporeal body as you have.*

The same holds true for our spirit and how we choose to think and act. Our civilization seems to think that freedom of thought and action somehow nullifies our responsibility to govern ourselves in ways that allow us to become an asset to the world, not a liability.

Purity, wisdom, and goodness have been relegated to an antiquated and simplistic perspective of narrow-minded religions:

> *Even so, in regard to your spirit, your soul, your mind, your ideas and your thoughts, I gave you liberty in the same way.*
>
> *I gave you liberty to receive your inspiration from drunkards and harlots and fighters; or from people of wisdom, or the innocence of childhood, or the virtue of a virgin.*
>
> *Or from a city of corruption, or from the country, with pure air and trees, and flowers and mountains and valleys.*

As the Creator asks us to serve each other, so He also serves us according to our desires:

And I spoke to your soul, saying: Choose what you want to be the inspiration of your mind and spirit and soul; behold, I, your Creator, am your servant to impregnate you with thoughts and ideas and disposition. All you have to do is to choose.

It is all about choice. When a child comes of age, we cannot tell them what they must do. We can try to inspire them, but they must make the choice:

And, now, because I gave you this extreme liberty, and you have chosen, behold, you art accountable to yourself for your every thought and idea; and for your spirit and soul, and in your behavior you are responsible to all the world.

With liberty I bestowed responsibility also. Choose your own food, and your own raiment and your house; and choose the place, and provide the way for whatever inspiration you may, still you will be responsible in all; and the result will be to you according to your own choice, whether you fawn upon Satan, or emulate your Creator.

We are coming of age and we cannot avoid our own personal responsibility for who we are, how we act, and what we think.

The Calendar of the Seasons- Chapter XIV

It is time to regain our relationship with the cycles of life through living by the true calendar of the earth. The earth's calendar goes by the quarters of the moon as did the calendars of old.

The northern line of the sun will be the end of the year, and it will be called the last day of the old year, said Jehovih.

And the first day thereafter, when the sun starts on his southern course, will be the beginning of the year, and it will be called the New Year's day.

These are My times of the end and the beginning of a year, which I created;
and I made the earth and the sun as My written testimony of this.

How can we live by a totally different calendar when the rest of the world is living by a different calendar? Use the common calendar to mark the days and celebrate the Sabbath by the quarters of the moon. The Mayan calendar is one of several good examples of mapping out the days of year by the cycles of the moon. Here is their website: http://lawoftime.org

The moon calendar is another piece of humanity's coming together with each other and the heavenly worlds. When we live by the cycles of nature, we fall into concert with all the worlds:

And it will come to pass that the Sabbath days all around the world will
be the same day for all people, even with the travel of the sun. Therefore,
Jehovih's heavenly kingdoms will be in concert with mortals, as to times
and seasons in all things.

The Four Sacred Days

The sacred days are times when the spiritual worlds and the mortal world can celebrate together:

And Jehovih said: That mortals and angels may live and labor in
concert, behold, I have given certain days, where large congregations
on earth may be met by My organic heavens, in re-union, mortals and
angels, for the happiness of both, and for the glory of My works.

Chapter XV, Holy Covenant Day, the signing of the Constitution of
the United States of America on September 17, 1787

Chapter XVI, Es Day on March 31, 1848, when the veil between this
world and the next was pulled aside to allow the spirits of the dead, or
angels, to communicate clearly with mortals and vice versa.

Chapter XVII, Freedom's Day on January 1, 1863, the celebration of the freeing of the slaves by Abraham Lincoln when he signed the Emancipation Proclamation and truly declared this country the land of the free.

Chapter XVIII, Holy Kosmon Day, which is the day to celebrate our coming of age and the changing of the worlds. We do not yet know the date of this day.

Holy Kosmon Day

The last chapter in the Book of Inspiration has a lot to say about how our thoughts and actions affect our lives:

When you make and keep your corporeal body pure and clean, My angels, who are pure and clean, come to you to aid you, and to enlighten you.

And when you put away all unclean thoughts and all selfish desires, and seek to obtain wisdom, and to learn how best you can help your fellow-man, behold, My angels of light and wisdom come to you, and, by virtue of their presence, which you see not, they inspire your soul in the light of your Creator.

Man steps in and declares his freedom to make his own choices by himself:

Man has said: I will not be a seer, or a prophet, or a su'is, or sar'gis; verily, I will not have angels with me to teach me, or to give me any light or knowledge under the sun.

Whatever I can attain, it will be my own. Wiser is it for me to obtain to know, and to do things of myself, than have angels come and give to me, or manifest through me.

Verily, I will not be used, by Man nor angel, for it would be prostituting my flesh and my spirit to others.

Behold, my body was given to me for my own use and profit, to establish and develop my own soul to eternal happiness in individuality.

We can live our lives as we want and the Creator will be with us:

Alike to all people is My Presence, said Jehovih. I am to the just and the unjust; I am everywhere, both, in darkness and in light.

The effects of our decisions will determine our access to the Divine and to the happiness and fulfillment we desire. It seems that the choice is always about should we choose the immediate gratification or the long term fulfillment that we are not sure of:

Because you are in darkness, you do not behold Me.
Because you are imperfect in flesh and spirit, you deny Me.
Because you are confounded with inharmony, you do not believe in Me.

He, who does not have an ear for music, does not discover a tune; even as he that is discordant denies My Person.

Our true essence is goodness. We have the innate ability to be good, noble and wise. This is our nature:

To the pure there is no selfishness, neither for earthly things, nor for their own flesh and spirit.

A pure Man is as a clear glass; he can see out of himself, and, so, perceive My angels and Me.

Through the pure Man, pure angels can see mortality as well as spirituality. Their presence inspires him to understand all things.

Because we cannot see or hear or touch a spirit does not mean they are not there. The laws of attraction still hold true especially in the unseen worlds:

As much with the Man that is not a seer, or a su'is, are the angels, as with those that are seer, or su'is, or sar'gis.

Because you do not see, nor hear angels, only proves your darkness, but does not prove the absence of angels.

To the dark, come the dark; with the dark, abide the dark, both, angels and mortals.

More is the Man of darkness ruled by angels, than is the Man of light.

The Creator has a plan and we are a part of that plan. Our destiny is extraordinary and profound. We can run from it, we can ignore it, we can hide from it but we cannot escape it:

Behold, I did not create you to fill any place in the entire world for your own self's sake. I gave neither your flesh nor your spirit to be yours only.

These, also, will you relinquish, saying: To you, O Creator, I give all; my flesh, my spirit, mind, and all my service; to be yours forever.

You will say: Appropriate me, soul and body, in whatever way you can, that I may do the most good to others, mortals and angels.

Until you attain this, you will not hear My Voice, nor see My Hand.

We are the children of the Universe. We have the potential to become one with the quantum field. We are immortal divine beings and we will grow into our heritage sooner or later:

As I gave away Myself, and thus created all things, so will you follow in My footsteps, in order to become one with Me. Herein lies the secret of wisdom, truth, love and power, time without end.

The Book of Discipline

Open your understanding, O Man, that you may discern the beauty and glory of heavenly places prepared by your God, Lords and guardian angels. For as we came up out of the first resurrection, which may be likened to a great medley, a noise and confusion of a mighty multitude, so we covenanted with Jehovih to make ourselves orderly, and a unit in growth, manifestation, expression and future development, that the place of the second resurrection should be nothing in common with the first.

God Speaks About Himself & Creator - Chapter I

The Oahspe was given to humanity to explain the workings of the heavens, the progression of life after death, and the relationship of angels to mortals. In the Book of Discipline, God explains more about himself and his relationship to the Creator, the angelic realms, and to mortals:

> *For as I am your elder brother, so will it be with you, to raise also in times to come, and look back to mortals and call them to the exalted heavens of the Almighty.*

God describes the Creator and points to Him as that which will light our way forever:

> *Nor is there an angel in heaven so high, or sufficiently wise to comprehend Jehovih in His entirety, or to see Him as you see your fellow Man.*

Creator is everything. Creator is the quantum field of everything, everywhere:

> *For He is within all; beyond and overall*
> *Being Ever Present in all places*
> *Doing by Virtue of His presence*
> *Quickening all the living*
> *Adorable above all things*

> *Even as the sun is to the light of day, so is Jehovih to the understanding of all the living. To contemplate this is the road of everlasting life, rising in wisdom, love, and power forever.*

The God of this world is not the Creator. He or She is a onetime mortal who has evolved to take on the responsibility of managing a world:

> *God and Jehovih are not the same one; no more is your God than what you will be in times to come.*

There is a progression from life on earth to the passing over into spirit, to the evolution of our spirit away from the earth, and finally becoming free of the earth and serving in the etherean worlds. This evolution is for all souls. It is our destiny:

> *First, mortality, then death, which is the first resurrection; such are the spirits of the dead—angels dwelling with mortals upon the earth, where they abide, some for a few years, some for a hundred and some for a thousand or more years.*
>
> *Second, angel organization in heaven, and their abandonment of mortals, which is the second resurrection.*

The God/Goddess of the earth is a being who has evolved from a onetime mortal to become capable of managing the heavens and the earth:

> *As a kingdom on earth has a king, and the king is nevertheless a mortal, so in like manner is the heavenly place of your God a kingdom of angels, and the chief over them is God, an angel also.*

We all wonder if there is sentient life on other planets:

> *However the kingdom of your God embraces all the heavens of the earth. So is it also with all corporeal worlds and their atmospherean heavens—a God and organic heavens belonging to each and all of them.*

When we have evolved into complete service to the Divine, we are sent out beyond the earth's vortex into etherea, which is the space between the celestial bodies everywhere. Our evolution is infinite and not limited to this world. *The Oahspe* has some wonderful descriptions of the etherean Gods and Goddesses who manage the roadways of the etheric heavens:

> *Nor is this all; for there is a third resurrection, in which the angels rise still higher in wisdom, love and power, and are sent by your God into etherea, mid-way between the planets—the highest of all heavens—over which there are Chiefs, who are also Gods and Goddesses of still more comprehensive attributes.*

More about the Heavens - Chapter II

A "parting of the veils" is happening on earth at this time. These "veils" comprise an energetic field between dimensions or worlds, and they cloak our mortal senses from seeing the next dimension. This separation between dimensions allows mortals a place to grow and learn without the constant awareness of the presence of discarnate souls. We have the ability to see spirits, but to see them all the time would be very difficult. This division of the worlds and dimensions works the same way for the spirits of the dead in the first and second resurrection. The heavens are divided into different densities to create separate places for the appropriate evolution of all the varied angels who live there.

When the veils are parted the first level of angels that are easily available are the earthbound souls who live on the earth amongst humans. Some are good and some are not:

> *Nevertheless, this also has been proved to you—that there are false angels and wise angels, as well as false seers and wise seers—and that out of the multitude of revelations from them, there has come neither harmony nor good works.*

Just like on earth, where there are good people and not so good people, and people you can trust and people who you should not trust, so it is in the spiritual realms. Just because a being is in spirit form does not mean they are enlightened or of superior intelligence. If they are earthbound they are not enlightened:

> *And it has been shown that the spirits of the dead possess for a long period of time the same characteristics and prejudices as when in mortality; and since there is neither harmony nor community of life among mortals, neither is there harmony nor community of life nor of teaching among the angels who manifest to them.*

> *For the angels through one prophet teach one doctrine, and through another prophet another doctrine, after the manner of the doctrines of the prophets themselves.*

You could think of life on earth as being in first grade. When you die, you graduate to second grade, keeping the strengths and weaknesses you had in the first grade. We are not instantly enlightened because we are no longer in mortal form:

> *Consider also the multitude of infants that die without any knowledge of either earth or heaven. And the multitude of unlearned, and foolish and depraved; for all of these as well as the wise and good enter the first resurrection.*

As in mortal schools, not everyone has the same aptitude or the same desire to learn. So it is in the first resurrection. Most of the beings that enter the world of spirit are ignorant and uneducated about spiritual reality. They are concerned with the same worldly things they were involved in on earth. As a result of this condition, there are many, many more spirits in ignorance in the first resurrection than there are spirits who seek to evolve spiritually:

> *And of the wise and good—who strive for continual elevation—how few, compared to the whole! Yet such is the relative proportions of angels of light and angels of darkness in proximity to mortals.*

The higher the consciousness of the angel, the further away from the earth they reside.

The Second Resurrection

As life on earth progressed and the heavens became more and more populated with discarnate mortals, it became clear to those striving to grow spiritually that they would have to remove themselves from the lower heavens in order to grow. And so the second resurrection came into being:

> Thus it came to pass that the wisest and best angels departed away from the earth; away from mortals, and away from the inharmonious presence of the legions of the spirits of the dead, and they inhabited a heavenly region by themselves.

The angels of the second resurrection organized themselves and covenanted to themselves, calling themselves the *Angels of Jehovih*:

> The chief of the rules was, that the angels of Jehovih should never manifest themselves as individuals to mortals, lest mortals become servants to, and worshippers of the spirits instead of the All Highest, Jehovih.

The guardian angels of mortals are only from the second resurrection. This provides assurance that mortals will be guarded and inspired by only the wisest of angels. As a part of this rule, these angels are only allowed to return to earth in large groups in lines of light or phalanxes. It is also interesting to note that the text says our guardian angels rotate in and out of service to mortals:

> Second to this—that when the angels of Jehovih should be appointed to mortals, it should be as guardians over infants, to inspire them by way of the natural consciousness within, as to what was right and good in

reference to eternal life. And that such guardian angels be in phalanxes of millions and tens of millions (but still in close membership with your God and his Holy Council) in order to relieve one another on guard.

Because of these rules of conduct for the higher heavens, it is easy to know from whom you receive inspiration. Not all inspiration from the lower heavens is negative, but it is usually self-serving:

For, by the inspirations of the angels of your God, the individual entity of a mortal is directed in its normal growth; but by the angels of the first resurrection, mortals are used abnormally, by entrancement, by miracles, or by sar'gis, oracles or otherwise.

Like Attracts Like - Chapter III

This is one of the best writings on spirit and mortal interactions, and how to distinguish where your inspiration comes from:

For alike and like Jehovih created mortals and angels to attract each other; and since the aspiration and desire of most mortals pertain to themselves as individuals, so the twain bound themselves in the same pursuits and earthly hopes.

For whoso on earth loved riches, or fame, or great learning or even evil, such as dissipation, drunkenness, gluttony, sexual indulgence, or theft, gambling or arson, doing any or all of these things for self's sake, or for evil, attracted angel companions of a like order, who, by inspiration or otherwise, led him on to achieve his heart's desire.

Our actions and desires attract spirits to us who have the same desires. They support us in the pursuit of our desires. We all like to have support and others to join us in our pursuits. This need does not change when we cross over into the next world, and, thus, earthbound spirits are attracted to mortals of like mind and heart. It has been said before in other writings that we prepare a place in heaven for ourselves by the way we live on earth. The caution would be to choose our desires and actions wisely for a happy and fulfilling life here and in the next world:

> *And it came to pass when such mortals died and entered the first resurrection; their former inspirers become their companions and rulers, having shaped their thoughts while in mortality through their labors for self and earthly objects.*
>
> *And these in turn became angel inspirers to other mortals of like characteristic, so that a long period of time passed away, before the spirits who were thus bound to earth could be persuaded there were other heavens open for them to come and inherit. And as it was so then, even so is it this day with spirits of the dead.*

How do the beings of the next world influence us? Do they whisper in our ear? Do they influence others to say things to us? Do they send us thoughts telepathically? Yes, to all of these ways of communicating. Our desires and thoughts are transferred from angel to mortal and from mortal to angel just by proximity. This can also be experienced with human-to-human interactions:

> *As cold metal in contact with hot metal changes temperature,*
> *so by angel contact with the spirit of Man, knowledge*
> *passes from one to the other. So also is it of the passions,*
> *sentiments, desires and aspirations between the twain.*

Because we like to have the support of other people around us, we tend to congregate in towns and cities. However, problems arise when too many of us gather in a city or a town. The areas of higher population are also highly populated with earthbound souls who contribute greatly to the pain and suffering of humanity:

> *As there are good lands on earth still unoccupied, while in other regions there are great cities with mortals crowded together, starving, and*

dwelling in misery, and they will not leave, even so is the great multitude of angels of darkness gathered together upon the face of the earth—and many of them will not leave into the higher heavens of Jehovih.

People tend to think of the next world, or dimension, as a place far away from the earth, a place separate and apart. Many of the spirits of the next world interact with us all the time:

Also, as where the sea breaks upon the land, and the twain are ever in contact, so is the spirit world ever in contact with the mortal world (which place of contact was named by the ancients the intermediate world or place of purgation, wherefrom none could raise till made organically pure).

How Do We Know What Kind of Spirits Interact With Us?

The main thing to remember is that the first resurrection starts near the earth. The earthbound souls are the closest to us and they come usually as a single person. The higher angels of the second resurrection do not give their name, they come as light, and they come only in groups.

Of the first, coming as individuals, whether professing names, signs or histories, and especially the ancients. Whose words are uttered from the standpoint of the earth looking upward?

But of the second, as light only. Whose words emanate from my holy places in heaven coming down to you.

Relating to an earthbound spirit is not necessarily a negative experience. They are often simply humans who have transitioned to spirit. They might be your former aunt or brother, or your former neighbor. The important thing to keep in mind is that a spirit is not necessarily a wise and advanced being.

Here are some more attributes of the higher and lower angels:

Of the first (lower heaven), flatterers, to win your favor. Whose counsel pertains to you and to earthly things?

Of the second (higher heaven), to teach you self–abnegation, and lead you to do good to others regardless of our own profit, caring little whether you are prosperous on the earth provided you will be raised up in times to come.

For the revelations of the second resurrection come from the light of my Holy Council, who have abandoned their earthly habits and desires, knowing the way of raising up everlastingly is by constantly putting away the conditions below.

> *Your God comes not as an individual; neither do my*
> *Lords (nor holy angels though they come in my name).*
> *I come in legions of thousands and millions.*

When a president of a country presents a new law, everyone in the country has the ability to hear about it, but very few people will see the president in person.

The responsibility of God is to teach us about the universal laws and what the repercussions are if we do not follow them. This statement does not come from a vengeful god, but from a kind elder brother giving us fair warning about the workings of the worlds and how to avoid deception:

I cry out, Order, Purity, Discipline, Justice and Good Works—or Retribution! O Man, beware of angels who say: In heaven there is no organization, nor God, nor Holy Council, nor discipline, nor order, nor teaching, nor self-denial, or, who say: There is no God, no Jehovih, no government in heaven or who say:

THE BOOK OF DISCIPLINE

- *There is no bondage after death; no place or condition of suffering.*
- *When you die your spirit will enter paradise and dwell in perpetual ease and glory.*
- *Heaven is an endless summer land, with silvery rivers and golden boats for all,*
- *Eat, drink and enjoy yourself for the gratification of your earthly passions, for when you are dead your path will be straight to glory.*
- *Heap up riches, for there is no punishment after death,*
- *Turn not your thoughts to your own soul to discover your ungodliness, for when you are dead your spirit will revel in bliss,*
- *The angel world is a place of progression without self-abnegation and good works,*
- *Behold me, I am from the highest, most exalted sphere, or from a far-off star,*
- *I have visited the planets,*
- *Resurrection comes by reincarnation—first a stone, then lead, then silver, then gold, then a tree, then a worm, then an animal and then Man, or that a spirit re-enters the womb, and is born again in mortality,*
- *Blessed are you; for a host of ancient spirits attend you - you have a great mission.*

For all of these are the utterances of the angels of the first resurrection. And though they may inspire great oratory and learned discourses, yet they are flatterers, and will surely lead you into grief.

The Influences of the First or Second Resurrection - Chapter IV

The following list of characteristics certainly gives merit to the phrase, "The meek shall inherit the earth." The second resurrection responses may appear weak beside the person who speaks from the perspective of self. Humility and service however are great strengths, as is a more universal perspective:

Of the first resurrection Man said: I know my rights and dare maintain them.
Of the second, he said: I ask not for rights for my own self; whatever is
put upon me, that will I bear.

If we are treated unjustly, how do we decide our course of action? Joshua would have counseled you to turn the other cheek. Non-resistance is a continuous theme throughout the Oahpse, as is having a desire to act for the good of all. This is a form of humility, which could be interpreted as a propensity to servitude. In actuality, it means surrendering to a greater force and discerning what matters most, over time.

When people tell lies about us, it is very hard not to respond in our own defense. This doesn't mean we don't tell the truth about our actions and provide evidence if asked, but we do not become involved in the conflict of debate:

Of the first: Let me justify myself in what I have done; behold, I am
falsely accused.
Of the second: Jehovih knows my case; neither will I plead in my own
behalf. Whoever is falsely accused let him wait; in time the Father will
right all things.

The desire for justice and liberty can be positive, but when it comes from only one individual's perspective without thought for the rights of others, it does not serve the greater good. Only with a bigger perspective can we truly accomplish the most for the most people:

Of the first: Let no Man try to rule over me; I will maintain my liberty
at all hazards.
Of the second: Since no Man in all the world has full liberty—why
should I ask it?

All of life is about perspective. How do we perceive our relationships with others? Who are we, and why are we here? We are God Seeds struggling toward the Light. We can fight with those around us for space, water, and food, or we can keep our focus on the Light and help each other:

> *Of the first: I have done my share, let others do as well.*
> *Of the second: Though I do all I can, yet I am short before the Creator.*

It takes a certain level of desire for understanding to drive us to ask the deeper questions.

When the desire to know outweighs the fear of knowing, we see ourselves and find our true nature.

There is no need to be afraid, because we are children of the Light:

> *Of the first: I will not consider my shortcomings, lest I be dejected in spirit. Of the second: Teach me, O Father, to look into my every act, word and thought, to purify myself in Thy sight.*

This last statement is very well known to many religions. It is a good thought, but a difficult deed. When we learn to see and understand each other's pain and fear, it is easier to turn the other cheek:

> *Of the first: Whoever injures me will suffer by my hand.*
> *Of the second: Let us render good to those that injure us.*

To Hear the Voice - Chapter V

God speaks to us about receiving inspiration from the higher heavens. How can we become more aware and more in concert with the greater body of beings that live in the many worlds around us, and with the Divine in all things?

> *Whoever rules over his own earthly desires, passions, actions, words, and thoughts, being constantly watchful for the highest light and greatest*

THE BOOK OF DISCIPLINE

good, is on the right road. And if they persist in this until it has become
a constitutional growth within them, then will they hear the Voice.

In a way, this says it all. Reach for the highest we can perceive and continue until it becomes a permanent part of us. Only then will we be clear enough to not forget in moments of conflict or desire. Our energy field will become high and pure enough that we can hear the Creator's voice.

What is the difference between someone who has become constitutionally attuned to the Divine, and someone who is still going back and forth between self and the desire for the Divine?

Shall the drunken man, reeking with foul smell, sign the pledge to drink
no more, and straightway say: We are temperance Men! And presume
to dwell with the pure? I say to you, until they are purified and grown
to be constitutionally temperate they are not temperate.

When we look to another person for wisdom or understanding, we should always consider that person's level of purity, wisdom, and goodness, and remember that our thoughts and lifestyles influence the level of angelic inspiration we attract:

Consider then the seers and prophets (who hear the angels) whether they
have grown constitutionally to be one with Purity, Wisdom and Goodness.

Shall a person inquire of the magician as to the inspiration of the prophets of
your God? Or the angels of the first resurrection be consulted as to their opinions
of My revelations, and their words taken for truth without substantiation?

Let all things be proved or supported by corresponding testimony known
to be true. As the holy person perceives how things should be in the heavens
above, so they are. The unholy person sees heavenly things but dimly; they
bind themselves in ancient revelations, which have become corrupted.

How do we become one with the Creator? To become aligned with the created universe or the quantum field, means to attune to life. By attuning to the Great Spirit in all things we will find ourselves:

> *Jehovih is as near this day as in the time of the ancients;*
> *put yourself in order, becoming one with Him, and*
> *no book so easily read as His created universe*

> *Inspiration comes less by books, than by what the Creator wrote—His worlds. Read of Him and His works. Frame your speech and your thoughts for Him. He will answer you in your own behavior and in the happiness of your soul.*

What does God expect of us? Is there a plan for where we are going and how to get there? What does God want?

> *It is the will and wish of your God, that all people become constitutionally capable of receiving and comprehending the highest light, and that they will no longer depend upon any priest, church, oracle or holy book, or upon consulting the spirits. That their behavior may make the earth a place of peace, with long life to all people, for the glory of Jehovih*

Jehovih's Kingdom on Earth - Chapter VI

We are in the time of Kosmon and this is the time when humanity will step into its higher potential and the world will live in peace. How do we step into our higher potential? The following list is about the attributes of those who follow the Light and those who do not, yet:

> *O Man, apply yourself to understand the spirit of my discourse, for in this will you find the key to the Father's kingdom.*

> *These are the rules of the second resurrection:*

> • *To become an interpreter and worker without a written formula:*

- *That whatever gives joy to your fellow and renders peace and good will to all—will be called light:*
- *That whatever gives sorrow to your fellow or discouragement to others—will be called darkness;*
- *As to find fault with another, or to aggravate to displeasure—will be called darkness:*
- *But to make another's burden light, to encourage them to strength and happiness—will be called light:*
- *To be forever complaining about this or that—will be called darkness:*
- *To be forever imparting cheerfulness—will be called light.*

We are often concerned about protecting ourselves from those who would use us or harm us, for surely the good people will be destroyed by the bad people if there is no protection for the good people:

Now therefore whoever becomes a member of my kingdom will practice light; but whoever practices darkness, will depart away from my kingdom of their own accord.

Neither will you practice darkness upon your fellow for any shortness they have done.

Nor will you reprove them for error, nor blame them, nor make yourself an inquisitor over them, nor assume to be a judge over them.

Nor ask them to apologize, nor otherwise seek to make them humble themselves before you.

Nor will you boast over them because you art wiser or stronger or more expert.

For all such inquisition comes of darkness, and will return upon they who utter it, in time to come.

Rather you will discover the good that is in your neighbor, and praise them, for this is the method of raising them higher.

A New Light and A New World - Chapter VII

Consider then what your mind will go in search of, that it may pursue the highest. This is serving the All Highest instead of darkness.

We have been taught to judge others according to how they look, how they act, and how intelligent they seem. Our judgments seldom serve to uplift and encourage them. We live our lives by making comparisons, which are usually not very kind. Now we are being asked to let go of our pettiness and separation, and serve the Light. How do we do this?

The All Highest in your neighbor, which they manifest—those perceive and discourse upon—all else in them, see not nor mention. The All Highest subjects—that discourse upon—all else pass by.

But now, behold, O mankind, I come to give a great religion, yet not to set aside the old; I come to such as do fulfill the old, and to give them the religion of the Gods themselves! Saying to them: Go save others, and no longer concern yourselves about yourselves.

What does this look like? Consider this quote from the Christian Bible:

'Therefore I tell you, do not be anxious about your life, what you will eat or what you will drink, nor about your body, what you will put on. Is not life more than food and the body more than clothing? Look at the birds of the air: they neither sow nor reap nor gather into barns, and yet your heavenly Father feeds them. Are you not of more value than they? And which of you by being anxious can add a single hour to his span of life? And why are you anxious about clothing? Consider the lilies of the field, how they grow: they neither toil nor spin, yet I tell you, even Solomon in all his glory was not arrayed like one of these.' Matthew 6: 25-34

One of the greatest things we can do to help others is to create places where people can learn to live together in kindness, cooperation and mutual respect. Spiritual communities can be created where people learn to live in peace and prosperity:

> *Go you and provide a place of second resurrection on earth, where the people will put away all low things and practice the all-highest.*

The main change that God asks of us is to relinquish our isolated existence and opposition to one another's perspective. When we move beyond our differences and work to help each other we can help to create heaven on earth:

> *Mine will not concern themselves as to their own self's salvation; for having faith in the Creator, that if they raise others up, with their own wisdom and strength, they are already saved, and without fear.*

We revere this practice in the great people of the world: Gandhi, Mother Teresa, Albert Schweitzer, Martin Luther King, all the prophets, and many, many others.

How do we choose what kind of people to bring into a community? Shouldn't we discriminate regarding whom we can help and whom we cannot help?

> *How does your God choose his initiates? Does he have censors? Saying to all who come—hold, be you examined and tried to prove you are worthy of the second resurrection? No, for this would imply inquisition—a court of darkness.*

The second resurrection, or higher heavens, does not discriminate regarding who comes to them:

> *Now, behold, O mankind, after the second resurrection was established in heaven, I called out to all the heavens of the earth, saying: Come, all you of the first resurrection, also, let my guardians go down to mortals and proclaim to all people—the kingdom of God is open to all who choose to come.*

The higher heavens do have rules by which they live. The gates of heaven are open to all who wish to live that way.

It is a challenging path to walk. The lives of Mother Teresa, Gandhi and Dorothy Day, exemplify the challenges a person might face. Look at what was accomplished by these courageous acts of selfless service. There is a fine line between discerning how we can help another person, and judging that someone cannot be helped:

> *Others said: What of the indolent and the shiftless? Will they not overrun us and set aside the good we aim at? And your God answered them, saying: When you practice the all-highest, behold the others will depart away from you.*

Knowing how to uplift another is a great art:

> *Nevertheless whoever has strength and yet will not support themselves - teach you one such person to change their attributes and you will be honored amongst Gods.*

When we put these words into practice and do our best to become aligned to the highest possibilities in ourselves, then we are aligning with the higher beings in the spiritual realms. This alignment will help us to accomplish our work:

> *Your glory is to fulfill the all-highest yourself.*
> *When all who can, will do this, there rest your faith that the quickening power and wisdom of Jehovih will sustain His kingdom through His holy angels.*

To Follow the Highest Light - Chapter VIII

We all have varying opinions about which path is the highest:

> Be considerate of your fellow Man, and weigh their standing place in the sight of your God. For one person says: My highest light is to get money; another, to get great learning; another, to enjoy earthly pleasures; another, to contemplate sexual relations; another, to serve Buddha; another, to serve Brahma; another, to serve Christ; another, to be efficient in warfare, and so on, everyone from their own standpoint.

How can we overcome the separation that occurs as a result of our different opinions? An opinion is an observation. It does not necessarily reflect the perception of a person's soul. It is a thing that changes as we change. It is an offering of a thought, not a gauge of the value of a person. Let every opinion stand on its own merit. Having an opinion and being willing to put that opinion aside in pursuit of proven wisdom is pursing the light:

> For which reasons you will explain that only facts well known, or comparatively proven, are light. An opinion is not light. That whoever professes light must know the matter of their own knowledge.

Some people think that because information comes from an angel or a spirit, it is higher truth. We are to question all beings, mortal and immortal, as to the merit of their information and not assume that a spirit has more wisdom than a mortal:

> Was it not the consulting of the oracles that destroyed Vind'yu (India), Socatta, Fonece (Phoenicia), Persia, Ghem and Greece? Such consultation of angels is answered from the first resurrection; and it ever will be so, save Man exact from the angel's facts and substantial proof.

The characteristics of the Light of Knowledge:

> *These, then, are rules of light: That which is self-evident That which is axiomatic That which is substantiated by facts That which has a parallel in known things That which leads to peace, order, and the uplifting of your neighbor and yourself.*

The end of the Book of Discipline gives a statement about how to practice the highest Light and a description of the practice of darkness:

> *Also to discipline yourself to be constantly on the alert to be pure, good, truthful and gentle in your speech; to practice right doing—these are following the highest light.*
>
> *This though is darkness—to express fault finding, criticism, censure, or even an opinion unsupportable by facts.*

The End of Eoih's Voice in the Wind

Conclusion

Much of the information in *Eoih's Voice in the Wind* has been given to humanity over and over again in many languages throughout the history of Man. We have reached a pinnacle in our evolution that has brought us to the edge of old ways of being and the beginning of new ways of being. We can no longer sit on the edge of possibility saying maybe tomorrow I'll change; maybe tomorrow I'll get a new job that makes me feel good about myself and my life; maybe I'll find some time later to help other people; maybe I can live a life with meaning and purpose; maybe this world is worth saving and people are not so bad – maybe.

The human race, has been allotted a certain amount of time to evolve to a level of understanding in which we can live a productive and happy life in peace and prosperity on a global level. Our allotment is up. Now is the time that we must step away from the limitations of the past and become the best of who we are. All life on earth is going through this process together. Species are becoming extinct and new species are being found. The world is in a state of metamorphism on a grand level. The earth Herself is making dramatic shifts and changes, like a sleeping giant awakening after a long rest. She is shifting and moving and melting and quaking and shaking up the world. We have to awaken with Her or become extinct. We have to start listening to the sounds inside us, the rhythms of our hearts, the thoughts and feelings and comments that we make to ourselves all the time. What are we saying? Who are we and where are we going? We need to listen to the sounds of life around us. Not just the sounds of the cities, but the sounds of the earth, of the birds, of the rain, of the ocean and the wind. Where are we going and how are going to get there?

We don't really have a map for tomorrow or next year. We all have plans for our lives, but are we paying attention to the larger drama of life itself that is playing out its destiny while we make our plans. When I say the larger drama I don't mean just the wars, the crimes, the hunger and poverty of humanity in general, but also the great unfolding of the earth and the solar system and the galaxy and the human heart.

If we can wake up each morning and take a few moments to ask Life how we can help, we might find some new answers that will take us into a better tomorrow. If we can pause before we go to work and ask the Creator how we can help, we might find our days more interesting and fulfilling. If we can look at each person we see during our day and know that they are a part of our family then our own loneliness and isolation can start to go away. If we could release one negative idea about ourselves we would be a little stronger and clearer. If we could release one negative idea about this world and replace it with a positive one the world would get a little stronger and better. Life is eternal and we can wait until tomorrow or when we die to become the fullness of ourselves, but we will have missed an extraordinary opportunity to shed our old skin and take on new wings in the light of all that seems to hold us back.

Eoih's Voice in the Wind asks us to step away from the drama and the trauma of the world and see the goodness and the beauty in ourselves, in our world and in each other. Helping each other instead of criticizing each other would be a good start. Living in peace and compassion toward all life align us with great forces of goodness. When we work to support a sustainable world for everyone, by living in harmony ourselves, we add to the greater good.

We are not being asked to make a few small changes in our lives, we are being asked to fulfill our human and spiritual potential to the best of our ability, now. We are being asked to live as truly advanced beings and participate in creating a world that works for everyone. We can learn to dance with the Gods, in fact we must learn to dance with the Gods, or perish.

May the wisdom contained within this book inspire you and uplift you and give you the hope and understanding necessary to lead you to happiness and a life of higher purpose.

Anne apRoberts
Abbess of the Order of the Trees

Oh, Great Spirit,
Whose voice I hear in the winds
and Whose breath gives life to all the world, hear me.
I am small and weak.
I need your strength and wisdom.
Let me walk in beauty and make my eyes ever behold the red
and purple sunset.
Make my hands respect the things you have made and my ears
sharp to hear your voice.
Make me wise so that I may understand the things you have
taught my people.
Let me learn the lessons you have hidden in every leaf and rock.
I seek strength, not to be superior to my brother, but to fight
my greatest enemy- myself.
Make me always ready to come to you with clean hands and
straight eyes, so when life fades, as the fading sunset, my spirit
will come to you without shame.

Lakota Chief Yellow Lark, 1887

About the Author

Anne apRoberts has spent most of the last 40 years living in the Oregon wilderness helping to create the Order of the Trees, a spiritual community modeled after the teachings of the Oahspe. She is presently the head of the Order of the Trees. She has been trained in herbology and many healing modalities. She is a gardener, a chief, and a jack of all trades.

Anne arrived in Oregon in 1975 at the age of 25. She wanted to help the earth by creating a way of life that would inspire others to live sustainably and find their connection to the soul of all things.

She is still living in the heart of nature and she wants you to know that it is possible to live sustainably and to deepen our connection to the soul of all things, every day.

She can be reached through our website at: www.eloinforest.org

Editor's Preface To The First Edition Of Oahspe, 1882

When a man holds up a book and says, "You must believe this, because it says, 'So said the Lord,' should we not pity that man?" Does he comprehend the liberty of Man to acquire knowledge?

Any book that imparts knowledge of the life and destiny of Man is a good book. Any book that unfolds the character and person of the Creator, and the wonder and glory of His creations, is a good book.

When a book gives us information of things we know not of, it should also give us a method of proving the information to be true. The day has arrived when Man will not accept proclamations and assertions; he wants plausible reasons, or substantial proofs, that the authority be not merely a pretense, but a demonstrable fact.

The time of Man-worship is at an end; readers no longer accept a book as good and great merely because any certain one wrote it. The book must have merits of its own; otherwise, it will soon pass out of existence.

If a book were to fall down from the sky with the Creator's signature to it, Man would not accept the book on that account. Why then should anything be said about how this book was written? It is not a destroyer of old systems or religions. It reveals a new one, adapted to this age, within which all people can be as brethren.

Epigraph

How Oahspe Was Written

The book of Oahspe was written through Dr. John Newbrough by the means of automatic writing. He was a dentist and a doctor, who became interested in the deeper questions of life. Below is his personal account of how he came to write the Oahspe. Some people tend to discount the authenticity of a text if it is written by means that are beyond the logical mind. However, many religious teachings have come through inspiration and (sometimes) miraculous events.

In the words of Dr. Newbrough:

Some two years ago, Oahspe was mechanically written through my hands by some other intelligence than my own. Many Spiritualists are acquainted with this automatic movement of the hands, independent of one's own volition. There are thousands and thousands of persons who have this quality. It can also be educated, or rather the susceptibility to external power can be increased. In my own case, I discovered many years ago that when sitting in circles to obtain spiritual manifestations, my hands could not lie on the table without flying off into these tantrums. Often they would write messages, left or right, backward or forward; nor could I control them any way other than by withdrawing from the table. Sometimes the power, thus baffled, would attack my tongue, or my eyes, or my ears, and I talked and saw and heard differently from my normal state.

Then I went to work in earnest to investigate spiritualism, and I investigated over two hundred mediums, traveling hundreds and hundreds of miles for this purpose. Often I took them to my own house and experimented with them to my heart's content. I found that nearly all of them were subject to a similar involuntary movement of the hands or to entrancement. They told me it was angels controlling them. In the course of time, about ten or fifteen years, I began to believe in spiritualism.

But I was not satisfied with the communications; I craved the light of heaven. I did not desire communications from friends or relatives, or information about earthly things; I wished to learn something about the Spirit world; what the angels did, how they traveled, and the general plan of the universe. So after a while I took it into my head that wise and exalted angels would commune better with us if we purified ourselves physically and spiritually. So I gave up eating flesh and fish, milk and butter, and took to rising before day, bathing twice a day, and occupying a small room alone, where I sat every morning half an hour before sunrise, recounting daily to my Creator my shortcomings in governing myself in thought and deed. In six years training, I reduced myself from 250 pounds to 180; my rheumatism was all gone, and I had no more headaches. I became limber and sprightly. A new lease of life came to me.

Then a new condition of control came upon my hands. Instead of the angels holding my hands, as formerly, they held their hands over my head. And they were clothed with sufficient materiality for me to see them, and a light fell upon my own hands as they lay on the table. In the meantime, I had attained to hear audible angel voices near me. I was directed to get a typewriter, which writes by keys like a piano. This I did, and I applied myself industriously to learn it, but with only indifferent success. For two years more the angels propounded to me questions relative to Eoih's Voice in the Wind, which no mortal could answer very intelligently. I always look back on these years as an enigma. Perhaps it was to show me that a man is but an ignoramus at best; perhaps I was waiting for constitutional growth to be good.

One morning, the light struck both hands on the back, and they went for the typewriter, for some fifteen minutes, very vigorously. I was told not to read what was printed, and I had worked myself into such a religious fear of losing this new power that I obeyed reverently. The next morning, also, before sunrise, the same power came and wrote (or printed, rather) again. Again I laid the matter away very religiously, saying little about it to anybody. One morning, I accidentally (it seemed accidental to me) looked out of the window and beheld the line of light that rested on my hands extending heavenward like a telegraph wire toward the sky. Over my head there were three pairs of hands, fully materialized, and behind me stood another angel with her hand on my shoulder. My looking did not disturb the scene; my hands kept right on, printing and printing.

For fifty weeks, this continued every morning, half an hour or so before sunrise, and then it ceased and I was told to read and publish the book Oahspe. The peculiar drawings in Oahspe were made with a pencil in the same way. A few of the drawings I was told to copy from other books, such as Saturn and the Egyptian ceremonies.

Now during all the while I have pursued my avocation (dentistry), nor has this matter nor my diet (vegetables, fruits, and farinaceous food) detracted any from my health or strength, although I have continued this discipline for upward to ten or more years. I am firmly convinced that there are numberless persons who might attain to marvelous development if they would thus train themselves. A strict integrity to the highest light is essential to development. Self-abnegation and purity should be the motto and discipline of everyone capable of angel communion.

J.B. Newbrough New York, January 21, 1883

Glossary

ANGELS:
>A once mortal being who is now deceased and living in the spirit world.

ARC:
>A section or designated space in etherea along the roadways of etherea, such as the Arc of Kosmon or the Arc of Bon.

ARCHANGELS:
>A once mortal being, now in spirit serving the Creator in etherea.

ANGELS OF DARKNESS:
>All spirits are below grade one.
>Earthbound souls.

DAMONS: (Origin of demon)
>An angel that usurps a mortal body and holds the original spirit in abeyance.

DRUJAS:
>Earthbound souls who are devoid of spiritual development.

ENGRAFTERS:
>A skilled fetal that claims to be a reincarnated spirit, moving from host to host after each corporeal body dies.

FETALS:
>Angels who engraft themselves on mortals. They feed on mortals for they lack spiritual knowledge and power.

VAMPIRES:
>Angels who nestle in the auric field of mortals, living on their substance. They often cause insanity.

A DU:
>The age when nothing can generate on a planet.

A JU:

The first degree of density of an atmospherean world.

ASHARS:

Angels appointed as guardians over mortals. They serve for 4 generations or 133 years

ASAPHS:

Angels appointed to receive the spirits of the dead into heaven.

A SU:

(Vedic) meaning Adam. The first race of Man. The A su lived upon the earth approximately seventy-two thousand years ago.

ATMOSPHEREAN WORLDS:

The spirit worlds or heavens. Sometimes called the next dimension.

THE BEAST:

The Beast is the selfish part of Man, the lower self.

THE HEADS OF THE BEAST:

False gods that set up false religions for the control of humanity.

BIBLE:

Any book or collection of writings constituting a sacred text. A book containing the authoritative writings of a religion. Any book considered authoritative in its field.

ORIAN CHIEF:

The overseeing God of a region in etherea. Perhaps the ones in charge of each galaxy.

CHIVAT:

The edge of the earth's vortex.

CREATOR:

See Jehovih at the beginning of the Glossary.

CORPOR:

The physical world. Matter. Considered positive or masculine.

CORPORAL:

Of the physical world of matter.

CYCLIC COIL OF THE GREAT SERPENT:

It is the time of the cyclic coil when Man makes a god of riches and supposed sciences and learning.

DAN HA:

A measurement of time from one time of light upon the earth to another.

DAN:

A region of light that the earth passes through on its journey through the cosmos.

ES, DAUGHTER OF JEHOVIH:

Spirit; the unseen worlds, etherea and atmospherea. The es of a living mortal is their spirit. It is called the daughter because it is negative, the receptive feminine.

ES EANS:

Those who live in the spirit world, a spirit, sometimes called an angel.

ES ENARS:

Angelic musicians composed of singers and instrument players.

ESFOMA:

Equivalent to there is something in the wind; or as things seem to indicate. Signs of the times.

ETHE:

The most subtle of all created substance. It fills all of what we call empty space.

ETHERA:

The highest, most rarified of the spirit realms. Beyond the vortex of this world and all worlds.

ETHEREAN:

One who lives in the spirit world above Atmospherea called etherea. One who has obtained a grade above 99 percent.

FAITHEST:

One who is dedicated to the Creator, having faith in the All Light above all things.

FAMILIAR:

Earthbound spirits who impersonate famous people.

GOD/GODDESS:

Is not the Creator, but our elder brother or sister in spirit who has evolved to a state of enlightenment in which he or she is capable of managing the evolution of this world. We use the word God throughout this text to mean God or Goddess. These angels also inhabit the etherean worlds.

GRADES AND RATES OF MORTALS:

The conscious growth of a human being is graded according to the development of their consciousness in selfless service. A person at grade 25 would be 75 percent for themselves and 25 percent for others. A person at grade 75 would be 75 percent for others and 25 percent for themselves.

The prophets were in the 90 percent.

The following forefathers were above grade 80; Paine, Jefferson, Adams, Franklin, Carroll, Hancock and Washington.

HA K:

Ignorance and darkness.

HADA:

The first heaven in atmospherea, closest to the earth.

HADAN SPIRITS:

The angels who live in the atmospherean heaven of Hada.

HEAVEN:

In general, the spiritual realms of the earth.

There are many heavens within the resurrections of the earth. These are plateaus or areas of specific consciousness within the spiritual worlds.

HELLS:

Places in the lower atmospherean regions where spirits are in chaos and madness.

HO TU:

When a planet reaches the age when it is past the time of begetting.

HORED:

A heaven of the earth, located in atmospherea.

I HIN:

A race of Man born of the union between the A su and the angels. The I hin was The first race of immortal Man. They are now extinct.

I HUANS:

This race were half-breeds between the Druks and the I hins. They were red like copper, taller and stronger than any other people of the world. They went down in darkness and were lost from the earth.

INORGANIC:

Denoting the heavens that lay upon the earth filled with earthbound wandering souls. Not living communally.

Wandering spirits that have not yet entered the first resurrection;

JEHOVIH:

Pronounced ge-ho-ve, The Creator, The Highest Ideal, the Nearest Perfect the mind can conceive.

KA YU:

Confucius. He was prepared by God to uplift the Chinese people. He produced twenty books which contained the digest of upwards of eighteen thousand books.

KOSMON:

An era, like the Age of Aquarius. It shall be called kosmon, because it embraces the present and all the past . It is the time when humanity comes of age or the age of enlightenment.

KOSMON ERA:

This era begins when all the earth has been inhabited; approximately 1850s.

LOO IS:

The masters of generations. Angels assigned to inspire marriages that will produce offspring that will uplift humanity and help in the evolution of Man.

LORD GOD AND LORD:

Angels assigned to assist the God or Goddess of this earth.

MAN:

With a capital is used to denote humanity, male and female and to stand as a reminder of the greater Man within us all.

OAHSPE:

A book received from the spiritual realms, referred to as a bible, a sacred text.

The word means earth, sky, and spirit.

ONGWEEGHAN:

Meaning good formed men. They came from the union of the I hin and the I huans. They had long black course hair, with brown copper skin. The Ongweeghan became a new race for they would not interbreed with the I huans or the I hins. They became the first flesh eaters.

ORIAN CHIEF:

An etherean.

An angel who has risen above the bondage of the earth and its heavens.

God of the Orian worlds that exist beyond the spiritual dimensions of this planet.

PAN:

> The name of a submerged continent in the Pacific Ocean that was sunk during the flood twenty four thousand years ago. See map in the back of this book.

PLATEAUS:

> Places in the spirit realm where the organized angels dwell, often called heavens. Their locations range from close to the earth to the highest region of this worlds atmospherea.

RESURRECTION:

> To rise from the dead, to bring back to life, to renew, to ascend.

> Levels of progression of a person and the progression of their spirit after physical death.

> The levels of ascension.

RIGHTEOUS:

> Virtuous and honorable.

SAR GAS:

> A materialized angel or a person in whose presence the angels can take on the semblance of mortal forms by drawing from the mortal's energy.

SE MU:

> The first substance used to bring forth life upon the earth.

SIN:

> To go against the Creator

SPIRIT:

> Your individual spark of the Divine.

SOUL:

> The presence of the Creator within you.

UZ:

> The vanishing of things seen into things unseen.

> Worldliness or the world's people.

UZIAN:

Signifies destroyer, one who is aligned to worldliness and not the spirit of all things, which is the Creator.

VORTICES AND VORTEXES:

A vortex is an etherean whirlwind that drives matter and energy toward the center producing form, from planets to people and trees, etc.

VORTEXIA:

The power of a vortex; the motion or field of a vortex.

Index

Resources

The *Oahspe* can be purchased from several sources on the web and through bookstores. The ones that have been updated into modern English are the easiest to read. You can read the Oahspe online and download a copy.

www.OahspeStandardEdition.com
www.StudyofOahspe.com

Life on Other Worlds by Anthony Borgia is the best account of life in the spirit worlds that we have found.

The Betty Books by Stewart White are an excellent series on communication between the worlds.

Proof of Heaven by Even Alexander, M.D. Dr. Alexander has a profound near death experience that changes his life forever.

The Lost History of the Little People by Susan B. Martinez, Ph.D. A wonderful history of our ancestors. Dr. Martinez weaves Oahspe's history of humanity with the facts of modern anthropology.